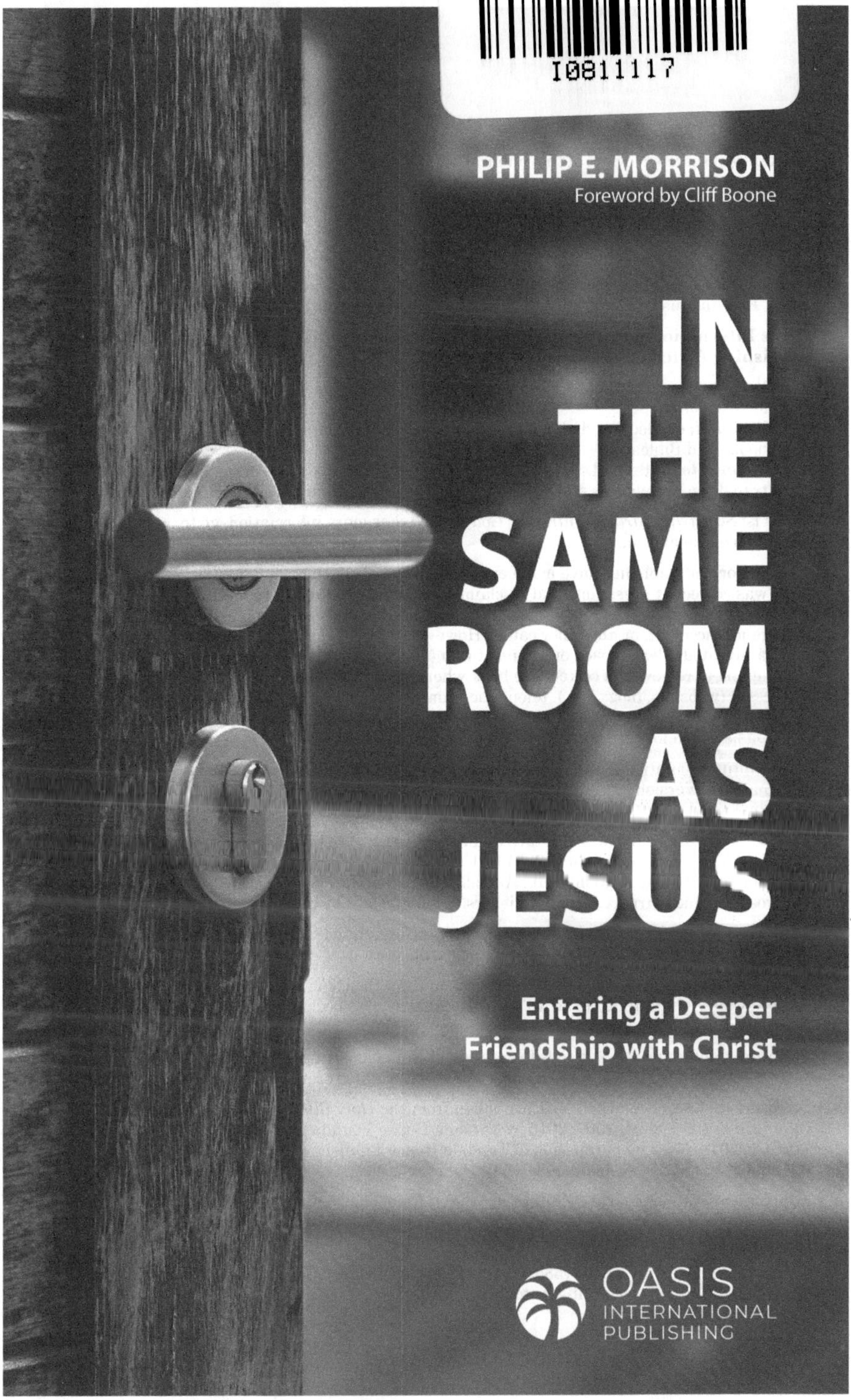
PHILIP E. MORRISON
Foreword by Cliff Boone
IN THE SAME ROOM AS JESUS
Entering a Deeper Friendship with Christ
OASIS INTERNATIONAL PUBLISHING

In the Same Room as Jesus: Entering a Deeper Friendship with Christ

ISBN 13: 978-1-59452-874-3
ISBN: 1-59452-874-8

Published by Oasis International Ltd, in partnership with Phil Morrison. To find out more about Phil and his ministry, contact him at philjanmorrison@gmail.com.

Oasis International is a ministry devoted to growing discipleship through publishing African voices.

- We ***engage*** Africa's most influential, most relevant, and best communicators for the sake of the gospel.
- We ***cultivate*** local and global partnerships to publish and distribute high-quality books and Bibles.
- We ***create*** contextual content that meets the specific needs of Africa, has the power to transform individuals and societies, and gives the church in Africa a global voice.

Oasis is: *Satisfying Africa's Thirst for God's Word.* For more information, go to oasisinternational.com.

Printed in USA.

24 25 26 27 28 29 30 31 32 TPS 10 9 8 7 6 5 4 3 2

Are you seeking a deeper life with God? A more intimate relationship with Jesus? You are not alone. Phil Morrison is on the journey with you seeking to draw closer to Jesus, who always seems as near as the next room. Go with Phil as together you "turn the doorhandles" that open the way into the life you are longing for.

– Mark Beazley,
Spiritual Director and MA Spiritual Formation

Do not read this book – unless you have a burning desire to experience and to love the risen Lord Jesus in fresh and real ways.

As I read Phil Morrison's small book, I was moved by how authentic this humble, transparent brother is. Phil shares his deepest thoughts and feelings with us. But *In the Same Room as Jesus* is grounded in Scripture, practical, and real – not ethereal. Digesting Phil's thoughtful guidance I appreciated very much that his wisdom is deeply grounded in the riches of the "communion of saints." He quotes extensively from many diverse voices in our rich heritage, including A. W. Tozer, Augustine, Richard Foster, John Woolman, Thomas Merton, C. S. Lewis, Brother Lawrence, John Baillie, Ann Weems, Richard Baxter, Tish H. Warren, Dietrich Bonhoeffer, and more. Commenting on Psalm 119:58, Phil writes: "This is the impulse of a person who hungers after God and a personal intimacy with him. And he is doing it with all his heart! This is no casual effort. This is an intentional and deliberate searching for a closer relationship. It is done with all of his being."

That is exactly what Phil's book about doors is all about. Be prepared for a transformational journey – and read slowly in a quiet space!

– George Renner, PhD, former faculty member,
New Testament and Pastoral Studies,
Nairobi Evangelical Graduate School of Theology, Kenya

When reading *In the Same Room as Jesus*, I kept coming back to the famous Marin Luther quote, "we are all mere beggars telling other beggars where to find bread." If the bread we are seeking is finding the reality of friendship and intimacy with the Lord Jesus, Phil Morrison is the proverbial beggar whose discovery will help us to do that. In a thoroughly readable way, with both the wisdom of God-seekers throughout the centuries and the practical touch of personal experience, this work shows us how we can "turn the doorhandle" and enter the room of that wonderful life with Jesus.

– David Harrop, Pastor of Global Ministries,
Calvary Church, Lancaster PA

Therefore, I am now going to allure her;
I will lead her into the wilderness
and speak tenderly to her. (Hosea 2:14)

Our Eternal Lover lures us back regularly into his presence with anticipation and delight. It is not hard to honour this regular time of meeting, for the language of lovers is the language of waste. We are glad to waste time with God, for we are pleased with the company.[1]

The friendship of the Lord is for those who fear him.
(Psalm 25:14 ESV)

Thy presence is to me a treasure of unending peace.[2]

Dedication

This book is dedicated to all those who hunger and thirst for a deeper intimacy with Jesus.

Acknowledgements

I am completely humbled by the help that I have received from a number of people in the writing of this book. Of course, this includes many authors from the past and present who have travelled ahead of me in this spiritual pilgrimage. I am deeply in debt to them, and I am happy that you will meet some of them in the following pages. However, there are others who have had a more direct hand in guiding my thinking and shaping the manuscript into the book which you now hold in your hands.

First, of all I want to thank my wife, Jan, who lives with me and therefore knows my spiritual struggles and inconsistencies. And yet, over the many years of our marriage she has been patient with me as I have slowly and painfully grown in my spiritual life and in my desire to live in the nearness of the presence of Christ. Without her support, love, and encouragement I would not be where I am today.

I am grateful for my good friend, Cliff Boone, who carefully and meticulously read through one of the earlier drafts and made invaluable suggestions for order of content and clarity of expression. I am also thankful for his contribution of writing the Foreword for this work.

Another reader was my Spiritual Director, Mark Beazely, who prior to his working through the manuscript unwittingly helped me to shape my thoughts and encouraged me in my desire and journey into the same room as Jesus. Words cannot express my gratitude for his contribution.

I also want to thank my brothers at CROSSroads Bible Fellowship Church who interacted with the material at our monthly Men's Bible Study. Your interest and response was a great encouragement to me.

Finally, I want to thank my king, my Saviour, my brother, and my friend, Jesus, who always wants me near to his gentle and lowly heart and to live in the light and love of his presence. His drawing love is why I have written this book as it is a testimony to his amazing grace.

Contents

Foreword

This book has the touch of God upon it.

Perhaps that is all that needs said but let me explain why I think it is so. My heart was deeply moved, and my conscience was challenged as I read this book. This is one of those books which does not allow you to merely download it into your brain as an addition to your knowledge. It won't let the reader have a mere intellectual encounter with it. Don't get me wrong, it has plenty of content with which to interact. But it is much more than that. It is a scalpel in the hands of the Holy Spirit, and the willing reader is giving the Spirit permission to do surgery on their soul.

This book is a fresh presentation of necessary truth. Each generation needs to use its own voice in articulating old truth. But the best of those voices does so in a way that brings the listener over the old ground without them yawning – without the "I already know about this" syndrome. That is what Phil Morrison does. You will find ideas in this book which are new to you but that is not the sole explanation of this book's power. It is powerful because it ushers you into the dynamism of truth you have heard about in the past but, for one reason or another, has lost its effect upon you.

This book shares a unique characteristic with David McIntyre's classic, *The Hidden Life of Prayer*. John Piper described that book as a "jewel-strewn tapestry." McIntyre was able to use copious quotations from other writers in a way that infused his little book with the life and wisdom of the ages yet did not make the reading experience clunky and difficult. Phil Morrison has managed to do the same. The reader is edified and stretched and blessed and refreshed with the wisdom and insight that God has given many of his children over the years and in various parts of his church. The work of the Spirit in the universal church is funnelled your way in this book.

I do not profess to have any special insight or revelation concerning God's movement in our time. I am but one person, living in one place. Having said that, I do believe that I am observing a movement of the Spirit in our day. There is a spiritual restlessness, a dissatisfaction with what is being experienced in our churches, a thirsting for more intimacy with God amid the noise and hurried lives of our digital age. It seems to me that God is using various individuals from various backgrounds to call our attention to the present obstacles we face as well as the way around those obstacles. There is no human orchestration involved in these calls. They are being made by people who are organizationally unrelated to each other. They don't even know each other, yet they are all calling us to the same thing. I believe that this book is one of those calls. It is a part of what God is doing in our day.

This book has the touch of God upon it.

– Dr Cliff Boone, author of *Christ Victorious*

Preface

Thou art the inviting One . . .
Let us never . . .
cease to respond to thy invitations.
– Arthur Bennett[3]

This book is written in the same spirit as that of the apostle Paul who wrote, "I do not consider myself to have 'arrived', spiritually, nor do I consider myself already perfect. But I keep going on, grasping ever more firmly that purpose for which Christ grasped me" (Philippians 3:12, Phillips). The church father Augustine writes humbly in a letter to Darius concerning his *Confessions*. He asks, "As, then, you find me in these pages, pray for me that I shall not fail but that I may go on to be perfected. Pray for me, my son, pray for me!"[4] I can only echo these sentiments and writing such a book in any other spirit would be audacious, if not arrogant. Who am I but a novice in the way of spiritual disciplines? I was heartened to see Richard Foster, the author of *Celebration of Discipline* and other books on spiritual life, confessing the same feelings when he wrote, "I am now speaking beyond my own experience . . . This last step is a little too big for me right now."[5] Which really is the truth for all of us who are seeking to draw nearer to the Lord isn't it? As C. S. Lewis wrote, "The truth is, I haven't any language weak enough to depict the weakness in of my spiritual life."[6] But that is not discouraging. When we admit our weakness to others, it means that we can begin our searching and seeking together with a great crowd of spiritual pilgrims. We are not alone. We are finding the way in community even though each one of us have our own special relationship with Jesus.

Why is another book on spiritual growth even needed when there are many others that have been written which tread the same path? These are questions I have asked myself even in the writing. The answer is twofold. Like some of my other work, this one started off for myself as a personal exercise, as I often process my thoughts and reflections through writing. Much of the material initially came from my journals which recorded my journey to a deeper intimacy with Jesus – a journey I am still travelling. But secondly, as I began to share my story and how God drew me into what I call a *relational relationship* with Jesus, I found that others were desiring and looking for the same closeness with the Lord. I found that what I was learning was helpful to them. And because of that I wanted to become another one in the long line of a beggar showing other beggars where he had found bread.

GOD IN THE THRIFT SHOP

God shows his sense of humour sometimes as he orchestrates the details of our lives. My wife and I recently moved into a new neighbourhood and we have begun to explore the thrift shops in the area. In one shop, I found Thomas Merton's *No Man Is an Island* and in another Richard Foster's *Prayer* and John Baillie's *A Diary of Private Prayer*. A fourth book was Ann Weems's *Psalms of Lament* which I picked up at a church's used book sale. I believe these books were providentially laid in my path as I renewed my journey to a closer relationship with Jesus. I freely acknowledge that I have included a large number of quotes from these and other authors. I view them as pieces of coloured glass each of which contributes to the unified whole of the mosaic which I am trying to describe in this book. Perhaps, these quotations can be viewed somewhat as a small anthology. It is my hope that their inclusion will be beneficial to the reader as they synthesize and clarify what I have been discovering in my spiritual journey.

One other book needs to be mentioned: Arthur Bennett's collection of Puritan prayers, *The Valley of Vision*. Bennett does not identify specifically the author of the prayers so I generally indicate it is "the Puritan" who has written when I quote from this book.

One of my concerns in writing this book is that it is so individualistic. It is centred on one's personal relationship with Jesus. But although I firmly believe that the spiritual life, of necessity begins with the individual, it must be lived and worked out within community, within the body of Christ which can "encourage one another daily . . . so that none of you may be hardened by sin's deceitfulness" (Hebrews 3:13). Dietrich Bonhoeffer writes:

> The Christian needs another Christian who speaks God's Word to him. He needs him again and again when he becomes uncertain and discouraged . . . He needs his brother man as a bearer and proclaimer of the divine word of salvation. He needs his brother solely because of Jesus Christ. The Christ in his own heart is weaker than the Christ in the word of his brother; his own heart is uncertain, his brother's is sure.[7]

Therefore, the Christian life, although it may contain times of solitude is not meant to be lived in isolation. Too often, I have lived that way, and it only leads to mediocrity or a false and deluded view of where I am spiritually. Thus, my encouragement to the reader is to find someone to travel with you on your spiritual journey. If you cannot find a fellow pilgrim, at least find a trusted friend with whom you can share your experiences of struggles and joy. It will help you stay committed and on course.

Sue Spencer's book, *African Creeks I Have Been Up*, is a delightful and insightful record of her family's West African journeys and adventures in work, life, and the parenting of her three rambunctious preteen boys with her mining engineer husband. What is striking in all this cross-cultural newness is her teachable spirit and learner's attitude which was expressed in these simple words, "I have so much to learn."[8]

And so, do I.

Philip E. Morrison, Psalm 115:1; Psalm 119:112.
New Holland, Pennsylvania
January 2021

Introduction

Jesus in the Next Room

No longer do I call you servants . . .
but I have called you friends.
(John 15:15, NKJV)

Teach me that genuine love is different in kind
from that wrought by rational arguments.
– Arthur Bennett[9]

I have always struggled with the friendship aspect of my relationship with Jesus. I have never felt it. I have rarely felt close to Jesus. Perhaps I was afraid of the commitment it might require. Or maybe it was because I didn't really know how to be a friend with Jesus. What I do know is that I have felt an ache and the longing for the closeness of a friendship with him, but I haven't been able to draw near. It seems like he is always in the next room – and I can't get there. But . . . I never felt a close intimacy with Jesus, relationally or emotionally. A. W. Tozer describes my experience in this way:

> Is it not true that for most of us who call ourselves Christians there is no real experience? We have substituted theological ideas for an arresting encounter; we are full of religious notions, but our great weakness is that for our hearts there is no one there.[10]

Sadly, for most of my life my relationship with Jesus has been devoid of the emotional. I believe this was due to the fact that in my personal life I had walled off myself from the emotional as a protective coping mechanism. However, as God led me into the ministry of child safety and protection, and I began to interact with abused children and survivors of abuse, I could no longer simply deal with it on the intellectual level. My heart began to be torn apart with what I learned, heard, and encountered. God began to allow me to feel compassion for these who had been violated and traumatized.

What I didn't realize was that this transformation in my emotions was opening up the door to spiritual wholeness and wellness. A. W. Tozer speaks to this when he writes:

> Our ability to feel is one of the marks of our divine origin. We need not be ashamed of either tears or laughter. The Christian stoic who has crushed his [or her] feelings is only two-thirds [human]; an important third part has been repudiated.[11]

Thus, for years as a Christian stoic, I had mostly an intellectual or cerebral relationship with the Lord. I believed Jesus was my Saviour and I worshipped him. I trusted his work on the cross. I have no doubt I am his child. I have tried to obey. These are all good but do not satisfy the need for intimate relational closeness. My experience was like the description made by Timothy Muldoon of many people today. He says, "What is so utterly foreign to many is the experience of falling in love with God. Religion, for them, is an intellectual exercise rooted in the individual conscience, rather than a response to a God who holds out a hand to say, 'Let's have an adventure!'"[12]

So, when trying to love God with all my being I have loved God with my mind in my studies, writing, and ministries. I think to a lesser degree, I have loved God with my soul in my acts of worship. But to love God with my heart – in that emotional and relational way – not so much. In the words of A. W. Tozer, my relationship has been "brain-deep, not life-deep."[13] I have missed out on a great adventure with Jesus as my friend.

When we speak of friendship with God, we cannot ignore a strong paradox in our relationship with him. We are to fear God, to approach him with reverence and awe on one hand. And yet, on the other, Jesus describes himself as our friend. If fear is primary, we will be too afraid to draw near. If friendship is primary, our relationship will degenerate into casual familiarity. A spiritually healthy relationship with God requires both and they must be held in dynamic tension.

So how does one relate to a friend one cannot see, hear, or touch? I didn't really know. It has become my quest. How I embark on a quest is through reading, thinking, and writing out my thoughts which is, admittedly, an intellectually oriented activity. But this activity also forces me to record what I have discovered and the path I have travelled and my experience as I have moved towards Jesus in the next room.

This is what this little volume is all about. It is a record of my adventure of opening the door of the next room and moving closer to Jesus. A lot of this is not new. Men and women have been moving towards Jesus for all of church history. But as I have been sharing my story and how I am growing in my relational relationship with Jesus, I have found that it resonates with others. They are in the same room as I have been and distanced from Jesus in their relationship. These are godly, earnest believers who are seeking to serve God and honour him with their lives. And yet they feel something is missing. They are intellectually sound but relationally empty. J. I. Packer clearly captures this truth in his classic work *Knowing God* when he writes, "We must not lose sight of the fact that knowing God is an emotional relationship, as well as an intellectual and volitional one, and could not indeed be a deep relationship between persons if it were not so."[14]

This book looks at various ways to enter into the same room with Jesus. I use the metaphor of doors which open into the room. As with any metaphor or analogy the imagery can be stretched too far and pressed into ways and meanings beyond what is true or helpful. So, I have reigned in my imagination and impulses not to make it bear more weight than it is able.

This is simply a record of my experience as I have been turning the door handles to gain access into a deeper relationship with Jesus. The Church Father, John Chrysostom encourages us to "Find the door of your heart, you will discover it is the door to the kingdom of God."[15] The kingdom of God is where the king is. So, to put it in terms of the picture I am using, we could say, "Find the door of your heart and it will lead you to the room where Jesus is." I am thankful that God helped me to find the door to my heart so that I could find Jesus. Not find as my Saviour, but to find him as my friend. Not to find him intellectually, but to find him relationally.

Obviously, we are speaking of experiential Christianity here. However, we must be careful that our personal experience, because of its subjective nature, is not made into an absolute standard of truth. Thus, while we are talking about entering into the presence of Jesus, we cannot base the truth of this solely on our personal experience or the feeling of his nearness. We will deal with the experience of feeling that God is absent in another chapter but for now we want to emphasize that even when we do not feel God's presence, we know he is with us because of the doctrine of God's presence as found in Scripture. Ray and Anne Ortlund write:

> Practicing God's presence, unless it flows out of the nourishing, deep-rooted truth of our Christian faith, becomes purely experiential, shallow, and eventually silly.[16] . . . Confidence in the rock-solid promise of his continual presence (Matthew 28:20) is what will strengthen and steady you in the down times when you feel nothing at all. Know the doctrine! You can always trust sound doctrine; you can't always trust experience.[17]

There are many doors into the same room as Jesus. I have explored a few in this book and hope in the future to find more. But not all of these doors may be for everyone, or at any particular time. God deals with us as individuals and as the infinite Creator he who has designed us uniquely is not limited to one means of access. My experience is that I have tried turning various door handles, but which seemed locked for me in the past. Now they have turned under my hand. So, if while reading this book some door handles do not yield as you turn them, it is okay. Perhaps they will open later on in your spiritual pilgrimage. What is important is that each of us seek the presence of Jesus in a mutual exploration and growth of our friendship and companionship with him. It is wrong for us to reduce our relationship to a formulaic one-size-fits-all approach. As Richard Foster says, "We can never dictate the means of God's grace."[18]

Perhaps you have, like me, been trying to live your life *for* Jesus. This has been the unstated focus of my life. As a young person at youth rallies, we would sing "Living for Jesus a life that is true. Striving to please him in all that I do."[19] What did that mean to me? It was to serve him, obey him, honour him, and build his kingdom. These are all good and essential aspects of a true believer's life. However, I have come to believe that there is more to the Christ follower's life than these intellectual and activity-oriented concerns. The focus was on what I was doing for him. Now, without neglecting these, I want to live *with* him.

In Luke 10:38-42 we have the familiar story of Jesus visiting the home of Martha and Mary. We find Martha very busy doing good things as she prepared the meal *for* him and all of the disciples and those who may have been traveling in his entourage. They needed to eat and be refreshed and by all standards of mid-Eastern hospitality Martha was doing the right thing. She was living *for* Jesus.

But Mary was *with* Jesus in the next room, and he commended her by saying she had chosen "what is better." Verse 39 could be translated, "She had a sister called Mary who also sat at the feet of Jesus listening." I believe this was significant. The word "also" could indicate that Mary had been in the kitchen working along with Martha *for* Jesus, but something drew her away from her preparation of the meal to be in the presence of Jesus. For her there was a time for service and a time for fellowship.

We must stop here and point out that if we are going to enter into the same room with Jesus, we must recognize the fact that it is going to take time. This is not something that can be rushed or done quickly. Therefore, we must choose to spend our time in his presence. Richard Foster writes, "We willingly "waste our time" . . . as a lavish love offering to the Father. God will then take what looks like a foolish waste and use it to bring us further into his [Jesus's] presence."[20]

Thus, the purpose of this book is to be a simple signpost to point out the different doors to the room where Jesus is. This is not necessarily a how-to book, although that aspect is present. Instead, my hope is that this an "encouragement to" type of book. Each chapter is not an in-depth exposition of each topic, but some practical guidance to help the reader explore how to walk through those doors into a deeper, more intimate relationship with him.

Madame Guyon says, "Your God is like a magnet! The Lord naturally draws you more and more toward himself."[21] Like Mary, I feel that drawing in my soul as well. My journey to this place *with* Jesus in the next room is the burden of this book. Will you come along with me to the feet of Jesus?

TURNING THE HANDLE

At the end of each chapter there will be a *Turning the Handle* section which will have questions for application for personal or group discussion to help readers to think about ways of opening the chapter's door and entering into the same room as Jesus for a closer relationship with him. Tim Keller writes, "We must not settle for an informed mind without an engaged heart."[22]

- As you begin to read and work through this book, ask yourself, "Am I ready to fully engage my heart in the pursuit of an intimate and relational relationship with Jesus?" If so, pray this prayer of commitment as the first step into the same room as Jesus.

  > Dear Father, Son, and Holy Spirit, you have created me for full fellowship with you. And yet, I know that often I am not ready to have an intimate relational relationship with you. I pull back; I hesitate to fully engage with you on this level.
  >
  > But now I feel you tenderly wooing my heart as I wander in the desert wasteland of my empty soul. And now, my heart's cry is "Lord, to whom shall I go? You alone have the words of eternal life. You are my only hope."[23]
  >
  > "My heart says of you, 'Seek his face! Your face, Lord, I will seek'" (Psalm 27:8). But I can only do this by your grace and through your strength. And now, I am committing myself to fully engage my heart in pursuing an intimate relationship with you.

1

The Nine-Door Room

The relationship between God and a man is more private and intimate than any possible relation between two fellow-creatures.
– *C. S. Lewis*[24]

In our apartment in Nairobi, we had what we called the nine-door room. It was in the centre of the flat where I had tucked a small desk for my computer. The living room, dining room, two bedrooms, a closet, a stairway, the shower room, the powder room, and the kitchen all had doorways which led into this room in the interior of our dwelling. To me, this is a picture of the interior of my being where Jesus, in the centre room, is waiting for me to enter. For us as we lived in that apartment, the nine-door room was always close no matter where we were. In the same way, for the believer, Jesus already indwells us. He is there; he is not far. He is waiting for us to respond to his gracious invitation. We are only a turn of the door handle away from being in the same room with him. And that is a joyous thought!

Throughout my life the journey towards Jesus has often seemed to be a pilgrimage – long, arduous, and fatiguing – with the destination far off and the arrival an unknown and uncertain reality. I think the view has been unconsciously influenced by John Bunyan's *A Pilgrim's Progress*. I needed to turn from that metaphor to my own of Jesus being in the next room.

Since Jesus is in the next room, in the interior of my being, how many doors open up to the place of fellowship? I have discovered some, which will be explored in this book, but I suspect there are many more which remain to be found. If this is true, then it seems that there is not just one way, or one door, to get to Jesus.

It should be stated clearly that I am not saying there are many ways of salvation when I use the nine-door room metaphor. There is only one way of salvation which is through faith in the finished work of Christ on the cross. In fact, Jesus says, "I am the door. If anyone enters by me, he will be saved and will go in and out and find pasture" (John 10:9, ESV). When we trust Jesus as our Saviour, we – God and us – establish the relationship.

Thus, what I am writing about is entering into a relational communion, fellowship, and life with him. We will enter into this intimate closeness with Jesus as we practice spiritual and practical disciplines which are represented by these doors that when opened will grant us access into the same room with Jesus. Some of these disciplines may be familiar while others may come as a new thought to the reader as we explore them in the following chapters of this book.

Andrew Murray, the South African pastor, author, and revivalist, wrote about the need for this fellowship with Jesus and its importance to spiritual growth and health. He said:

> The trouble with many Christians who try to believe and obey is that they do it in their own strength. They do not know that if the Lord Jesus is to reign in their hearts, they must meet with

> him intimately on a regular basis. Because they fail to do this, they do not really understand what it is to have fellowship with him.[25]

When we lived in Nairobi, to enter into most homes one had to go through an iron-barred gate and then a second door which had heavy locks. They were built to keep people out. One thing I am certain of, Jesus has not barred the doors into the room next door. They are left unlocked and unguarded. I see Jesus waiting there like the poet Henry Wadsworth Longfellow describes as he sits in his study and overhears his children gathering to rush into his presence:

> A sudden rush from the stairway,
> A sudden raid from the hall!
> By three doors left unguarded
> They enter my castle wall!
>
> [And when his children come in, he doesn't let them escape:]
> I have you fast in my fortress,
> And will not let you depart,
> But put you down into the dungeon
> In the round-tower of my heart.
> And there I will keep you forever,
> Yes, forever and a day.[26]

There are times for quiet, awe-filled, and slow approaches to the Saviour. But there are also the wild and childlike abandon of the child and friend who joyfully presses into the beloved's company. Such a time is this! Come with me! Jesus does not want to keep us out of the room. In fact, he is thrilled and delighted as he listens to our approach. Let us rush into his presence! He is waiting for us!

TURNING THE HANDLE TO THE NINE-DOOR ROOM

- A Warning! This book looks at many doors. However, we can only enter one door at a time in real life! Trying to begin too many disciplines at once may lead to frustration or disillusionment. Ask Jesus to impress on your heart which door or discipline he would like you to use. Begin entering through that door and as he impresses upon your heart another entry way into his presence you can begin to add that into your walk with him.

- Your response to this chapter may be, "At times, even right now, my heart is cold, and I have no desire for intimacy with Jesus even though I know I should." Admitting this is a good start because you are confessing your neediness.

- The next step is to ask God to give you the desire to draw closer to him. Richard Foster suggests: "Begin by inviting God to kindle a fire of love within you. Ask him to develop an ache in your heart. Then, when you are outside of his nearness for any length of time, this ache will begin again in you and will draw you back to his loving presence."[27]

  Why not start with the model prayer from the Puritan:

  O changeless God . . .
  My mind is a bucket without a bottom,
  with no spiritual understanding,
  no desire for the Lord's Day,
  ever learning but never reaching the truth,
  always at the gospel-well but never holding water.

My conscience is without conviction or contrition,
  with nothing to repent of
My will is without power of decision or resolution.
My heart is without affection, and full of leaks.
My memory has no retention,
  so I forget easily the lessons learned,
  and thy truths seep away.
Give me a broken heart that yet carries home
  the water of grace.[28]

2

The Door of Discipline and the Disciplines

Let me study and stand for discipline, and all the ways of worship, out of love for Christ; and to show my thankfulness; to seek and know his will from love, to hold it in love, and daily to care for and keep this state of heart.
– Arthur Bennett[29]

For some the word *discipline* may be a dirty word. It may conjure up hard and painful experiences. But that may be that those who see it that way do so because they are undisciplined in the first place. However, when we look at those who set and reach goals whether in athletics, business, or other pursuits, they inevitably practice discipline to achieve their goals. It is my belief that for us to enter into a life of intimacy with Jesus, we must discipline ourselves to take up our cross and follow him. Thus, in this chapter we will look at the need to have discipline as we practice the spiritual disciplines of the Christian life that will enable us to enter into the same room as Jesus.

Thomas Merton states: "To desire a spiritual life is, thus, to desire discipline. Otherwise, our desire is an illusion."[30] Walter Isaacson, the biographer of Leonardo Da Vinci puts it even more starkly when he says, "Vision without execution is hallucination."[31] And so we may say that we desire to be men of prayer like Daniel. We may say we have the vision of living holy lives and practice the presence of Jesus throughout the day like Brother Lawrence. Or we may aspire to fast and worship like Anna in the temple. But if we never take intentional steps to fast and pray, practice the presence or to live sanctified lives it is nothing more than an empty dream. A. W. Tozer says, "While the imagination races ahead to honour God, the will may lag behind and the [person] never guess how divided his [or her] heart is. The whole [person] must make the decision before the heart can know any real satisfaction."[32]

It is interesting that in many areas of life execution is lacking. Larry Bossidy and Ram Charan, although speaking of the business world, accurately describe the need for what they call the discipline of execution to accomplish one's goal or purpose. They write:

> Unless you translate big thoughts into concrete steps for action, they're pointless. Without execution, the breakthrough thinking breaks down, learning adds no value, people don't meet their stretch goals, and the revolution stops dead in its track . . . meaningful change comes only with execution.[33]

While these are words from the business world, and we don't want to make intimacy with Jesus simply a series of steps or of mechanically following a formula, there is wisdom in what they say. Many believers do not exercise the discipline of execution.

We may wish we could find the quick and easy way to a deeper relationship with Jesus. We want to find the three keys to spiritual growth so that we can follow a formula that will guarantee a short and painless entry into a close walk with the Lord. However, that is not to be. A. W. Tozer writes:

> No short cut exists. God has not bowed to our nervous haste nor embraced the methods of our machine age. It is well that we accept the hard truth now: . . . *who[ever] would know God must give time to him.* [We] must count no time wasted which is spent in the cultivation of his acquaintance. [We] must give [ourselves] to meditation and prayer hours on end.[34]

In a word, Tozer is talking about spiritual discipline as a way of spiritual life. Richard Foster, in his book *Celebration of Discipline* helps us get to the point when he says:

> Spiritual disciplines are things that we do. We must never lose sight of this fact. [For example,] it is one thing to talk piously about "the solitude of the heart," but if that does not somehow work its way into our experience, then we have missed the point of the disciplines. *We are dealing with actions, not merely states of mind* (emphasis mine).[35]

I believe many Christians have the vision of a close personal relationship with Jesus. We have a desire to walk in close fellowship with Jesus. But we never quite get into the same room as Jesus. While there may be various reasons, I believe that one of them may be simply a lack of following through on that vision and taking the steps that will lead us into the presence of Jesus. *We simply do not discipline ourselves to have or exercise the spiritual discipline.*

Where does discipline start? It starts with a commitment. David demonstrates this when he says, "*When You said,* 'Seek My face,' my heart said to You, 'I shall seek Your face, Lord'" (Psalm 27:8, NASB). The Lord's face represents his presence and David is stating his firm resolution to live in conscious awareness of it. Without an intentional decision and our heart set on entering into the presence of Jesus, it won't happen. Tozer calls it the habit of the soul when he writes about the results of making such a commitment when he says:

> God takes this intention for our choice and makes what allowances He must for the thousand distractions which beset us in this evil world. He knows that *we have set the direction of our hearts toward Jesus,* and we can know it too, and comfort ourselves with the knowledge that a habit of soul is forming which will become after a while a sort of spiritual reflex requiring no more conscious effort on our part (emphasis mine).[36]

It is like having the vision of being a great piano player but not having the internal strength or motivation to practice every day. Our dream or goal of performing concerts is an empty fantasy; it is only a happy hallucination. The same is true if we are not willing to practice the spiritual disciplines that Christians from the time of Christ to now have used to grow in their relationship with the Lord.

I know this is true, because I struggle with discipline in many areas of my life: my diet, my use of time, my exercise, and my leisure to name just a few. But I still feel the need, and I still keep trying to grow in becoming more disciplined. However, it comes in fits and starts and sometimes I can be disciplined for a while and then I slip back. It can be discouraging. Thomas Merton describing this struggle writes:

> If we are not strict with ourselves, our own flesh will soon deceive us. If we do not command ourselves

> severely . . . and make up our mind to keep our resolutions in spite of notable inconvenience and difficulty, we will quickly be deluded by our own excuses and let ourselves be led away by weakness and caprice.[37]

There are many disciplines in the spiritual life that will help us to grow. Some of which we introduce briefly in this book. But we need to be patient with ourselves and not try to start all of them, or put them into practice, all at once. It will be a quick way to failure and frustration. Like all things in life, spiritual disciplines are developed through habitual practice. Thomas Merton says:

> Discipline is not effective unless it is systematic, for the lack of system usually betrays a lack of purpose. Good habits are only developed by repeated acts, and we cannot discipline ourselves to do the same thing over again with any degree of intelligence unless we go about it systematically.[38]

So, what do we do with weakness in our discipline? I was discussing this with my son in one of our regular talks about our spiritual life. He said, "We have to have a plan. When I get off of it, I have something to go back to. The goal is not perfection in discipline, but the practice of discipline. And discipline in one area of life begets discipline in other areas." I believe this is a realistic approach. Instead of spiritually beating ourselves up over our lack of discipline, when we fall, we return to our original plan and desire and start where we left off.

I have been helped by the Northumbria Community morning prayer:

> One thing I have asked of the Lord,
> this is what I seek:
> that I may dwell in the house of the Lord

all the days of my life;
to behold the beauty of the Lord
and to seek Him in His temple.

Call: Who is it that you seek?
Response: We seek the Lord our God.
Call: Do you seek Him with all your heart?
Response: Amen. Lord, have mercy.
Call: Do you seek Him with all your soul?
Response: Amen. Lord, have mercy.
Call: Do you seek Him with all your mind?
Response: Amen. Lord, have mercy.
Call: Do you seek Him with all your strength?
Response: Amen. Christ, have mercy.[39]

What this prayer teaches us is that even though our heart's desire is to seek the Lord and live in his presence with all our being we realize we will fall short; we can't live up to what we profess with our lips. And thus, we cry for Jesus to have mercy on us.

So, how do we move forward? As we looked at the metaphor of doors, we acknowledged that perhaps not all the doors would immediately apply to everyone. The same is true for the spiritual disciplines. Thus, to be disciplined in the disciplines it is good that we pray and ask God to help us know with which one we should start. When that is clear we should then start small and grow into a consistent and habitual practice of it. And then when the Holy Spirit prompts us, we can move on to a new one as we grow deeper and more mature in our spiritual life.

To return to what was said earlier, the practice of spiritual disciplines must not become rote, robotic, or a rigid legalistic routine. We must guard against a quick default to doing the disciplines by sheer willpower rather than a dependence upon the Holy Spirit. We are not talking about a human-energized attempt to live the Christian life by doing practices which are on the list, rather than a freedom and empowering which is experienced by abiding in Christ's presence. In other words, there must be life, love, and liberty as we live out the disciplines in a gracious and intimate relationship with Jesus as we sit in the same room with him. Richard Foster writes:

> One word of caution . . . must be given at the outset: to know the mechanics does not mean that we are practicing the disciplines. The spiritual disciplines are an inward and spiritual reality, and the inner attitude of the heart is far more crucial than the mechanics for coming into the reality of the spiritual life.
>
> In our enthusiasm to practice the disciplines, we may fail to practice discipline. The life that is pleasing to God is not a series of religious duties.[40]

The Puritan prays:

> Keep me from fluttering about religion;
> fix me firm in it,
> for I am irresolute;
> my decisions are smoke and vapour,
> and I do not glorify thee,
> or behave according to thy will.[41]

TURNING THE HANDLE TO THE DOOR OF DISCIPLINE AND THE DISCIPLINES

- As you read through this book pay attention to your reactions to the invitations in each chapter and note which disciplines seem to resonate. Note the quality of what is stirred. What thoughts? Feelings? Desires? Pay attention to how they may be drawing your heart to be in the same room as Jesus.

- Richard Foster reminds us that disciplines are something that we do. This means that we need to choose what we are going to do and then make a plan as to how we are going to put it into practice.

  As you work through the disciplines in this book or learn about others, ask God to impress on your heart which ones you should put into practice. Then make it a study and plan how you will begin to introduce it into your spiritual life and walk with God. In this way, you will be "kept from fluttering about religion" and be "[fixed] firm in it."

3

The Door of Silence and Solitude

Understand – through the stillness.
Act – out of the stillness.
Conquer in the stillness.
– Dag Hammarskjöld[42]

One morning as I sat down for my quiet time with Jesus, I checked my phone and saw a message that my credit card bill was due in a couple of days. I checked my online banking app to see if I could schedule the payment before it was due, but it was not possible. As I turned to read my Bible, I couldn't focus on what was there. My mind and heart were totally distracted as I berated myself for missing the deadline and bemoaned the fact that I would have to pay a penalty. There was no silence in my soul. And because of that it disrupted my time of fellowship with Jesus.

As I am working on this chapter the world is in the midst of the Corona Virus crisis. In this time of enforced inactivity many are frantically trying to find things to do, to pass the time, and to keep busy. It seems we are addicted to our frenetic pace – to the rat race – to the adrenaline of activity and we cannot, will not, or are afraid to slow down, to be silent and to enter solitude. And because these worries of the world can choke the word (Mark 4:19, NASB), our relationship with Jesus is crowded out and diminished. Thomas Merton writes:

> Everything in modern city life is calculated to keep [people] from entering into [themselves] and thinking about spiritual things. Even with the best of intentions . . . spiritual [people find themselves] exhausted and deadened and debased by the constant noise of machines and loudspeakers, the dead air and the glaring lights of offices and shops, the everlasting suggestions of advertising and propaganda.
>
> The whole mechanism of modern life is geared for a flight from God and from the spirit into the wilderness of neurosis.[43]

And he wrote this just as television was becoming widely available and long before the internet was even thought of, let alone invented!

My children's band teacher would often admonish the audience at the school they attended to be quiet during the performance by summarizing Leopold Stokowski, "Painters paint upon canvas; musicians paint upon silence."[44] An extreme expression of this would be the avant-garde composer John Cage's composition *4'33"*. For this performance, the pianist David Tudor:

> Starts a stopwatch, sits down in front of the piano, closes the lid and begins a performance in which he never plays a note. After 30 seconds of silence, Tudor resets the stopwatch and times another two

> minutes, 23 seconds of silence, then another one minute, 40 seconds of silence.[45]

The music content of the composition was comprised of whatever extraneous sounds were heard whether it was crickets in the background, the movement of the wind in the trees, the breathing or coughing of the audience or their restless movement. This may seem strange, but the point is that these sounds would never have been heard, or if they were, they were never the subject of most people's attention.

Is it possible in our lives there are sounds – the whispers of the still small voice of God, for example – that we may never hear? Or if we do, they are not the subject of our attention because the many sounds and voices of the world around us draw them out?

Kevin Grenior says the same thing but uses a different metaphor:

> The presence of God is . . . hidden in plain sight. We find Him not by diligent struggle but through the clarity of vision that simplicity gives. He is seen through a glass dimly, but the light can indeed be seen, especially when all other lights – those things that compete for our attention – are extinguished.[46]

Is it possible that God is seeking to draw us to his light in this dark world, but we can't see it because we are distracted by the garish strobe lights of the world pulsating their beams into our being?

The point is whether in sight or sound we must simplify our stimuli to the essential, to the eternal wave lengths of our Creator that sympathetically reverberate within our soul. We are spiritual tuning forks made to resonate to the divine notes of God's love. We are spiritual prisms made to refract the light of heaven into the beauty of the rainbow so that all can see the glory of God revealed in our lives.

But we cannot vibrate to the voice of God if we are vibrating to that of the worries and cares of the world. They are not in harmony. They are ringing at a different frequency. We can only respond to the frequency of God when our soul's tuning fork is still. François Fénelon writes:

> We must silence every creature, we must silence ourselves, to hear in the deep hush of the whole soul, the ineffable voice of the spouse. We must bend the ear, because it is a gentle and delicate voice, only heard by those who no longer hear anything else.[47]

There is a time for making a joyful noise and praising the Lord with the sound of trumpets and loud clanging cymbals. But there is also time for quietness in the hush of the holy presence of Jesus. There is a silent worship because we have no words that can adequately praise and magnify the glory of God. Isaac Watts captures this in his hymn:

> God is in heaven, and men below:
> Be short our tunes; our words be few:
> A solemn reverence checks our songs,
> And praise sits silent on our tongues.[48]

Modern classical composer David Bruce speaks of the silence before a piece starts "as one of the most delicious moments filled with hope and anticipation."[49] So, if we choose silence as we come to fellowship in the same room with Jesus, it can fill our hearts with spiritually delicious expectant hope and joyful anticipation of warm intimacy with our friend. I try to make it a habit of not rushing into the room, but to come slowly, quietly, and sitting calmly in stillness in his presence. And often, sitting in the serenity of the early morning without the outside noise of the day's beginning, my inner being feels that he is with me.

THE FRAME OF SOLITUDE

As we begin to look at the many doors, or spiritual disciplines, that give entrance into the same room with Jesus, I believe that it is good to start with the idea of solitude as a frame that borders and gives structure to the other disciplines which lead us into his presence. Whether it is an hour, a day, or a week, it can still be organized in such a way that we will not fritter our time away.

Perhaps thinking of a picture frame could be helpful. The solitude would be the outer boundary of the time period. Inside the frame we could put a mat or even a double mat. A mat could be silence. Or it could be fasting. This would give further structure and enhancement of colour to the content, or the picture of our time.

The time would be the process of creating something new and we could use listening, meditating, reading Scripture, prayer, and writing as various colours on our palette and at the end step back and see what God's spirit has painted on the canvas of our soul.

We could picture it like this:

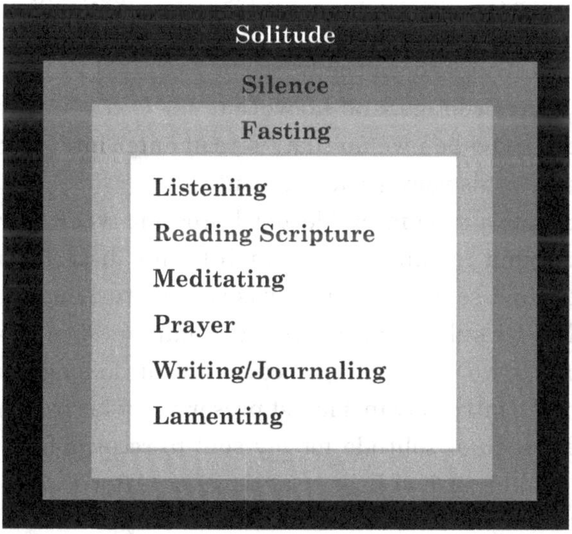

SILENCE AND SOLITUDE

Silence and solitude are not synonymous. But the two are often entered into simultaneously and by working together can be a door into the same room as Jesus. It is possible to be alone in solitude but not be silent. It is possible to be silent but not alone in solitude. Just as we have spoken about silence as a choice, so too is solitude.

Usually, solitude is for longer periods of aloneness and of silence. The benefit of this is that it gives us time to disengage and to untangle ourselves from our daily cares and routines. When we lived in Kenya in the 1990s, we would take a vacation near Mombasa on the Indian Ocean. At that time, it would be an eight-or nine-hour drive on a heavily travelled two lane road which was filled with potholes, narrow lanes, and washed-out shoulders. It was dangerous and intense. The physical sensations from the vibrations and jarring of the steering wheel would seem to last for hours after the drive ended. And it would take me a couple of days just to relax and unwind from that drive even though I was doing nothing but sitting near the ocean.

In the same ways, we need times of withdrawal from life's intensity and to unwind from the spiritual vibrations and jarring of our souls. We need, in the words of Psalm 46:10 to "be still" – literally relax or let go, and know that our God is God, and he is in control. And when we do that, we can enter into his presence, rest, and hear his voice speaking to us.

There was a time in my doctoral program where I was doing my background reading and research for my dissertation on the subject of child sexual abuse. It was very disturbing to my heart and soul as I would spend hours a day immersed in this horrific reality in our world. One day, I could face it no longer and went and spent an entire day in a forest preserve not far from my home. I needed the quiet solitude for my soul to recover from the jolting and shaking it had been experiencing. After that day, I was renewed enough to continue on with my study.

Thus, silence and solitude are means to prepare our hearts to sit quietly in the presence of Jesus after we have entered the room where he is. To hear Jesus, we must listen. And to listen we must be prepared to quietly wait as we invite him to speak to us. It is a process that cannot be rushed.

Ann Weems in "Lament Psalm Twenty-Three" writes:

> Speak to me now, O Holy One,
> to me, O God,
> the one who waits for your word.
> Speak to me so that I can
> return to life,
> and follow you once more.
> Speak, O my God,
> speak to me,
> the language of your heart.[50]

Tish Warren for Lent one year decided to start the day without spending the first five or ten minutes with her cell phone scrolling through Facebook and the latest headlines. Instead, she would use those first few waking moments with God:

> And I sat. At times, I'd read Scripture. Most often I'd pray . . . I'd invite God into the day . . . I'd lay out my worries, my hopes, and my questions before God . . . But mostly, I'd invite God into the day and just sit. Silent. Sort of listening. Sort of just sitting.
>
> But I sat expectantly. God made this day. He wrote it and named it and has a purpose in it. Today, he is the maker and giver of all good things. *I'd lap up the silence like mother's milk* (emphasis mine).[51]

It is not complicated. It is in simple choices and sometimes in small chunks of time that we can carve out stillness in our lives.

It is interesting to me that many, in the evangelical tradition, often talk of having a quiet time with the Lord as a time of devotion or worship. For a lot of my life, my quiet time was little more than reading the Scripture and then praying through my prayer list. Ironically, there was little time being silent in my quiet time. But now I have been practicing times of silence as I spend time with Jesus. This is how I seek to quiet every creature and myself and to be still as I enter the same room as Jesus so that I can hear in the deep hush of my inner being the loving voice of my Lord.

SILENCE AND COMMUNITY

One of my concerns is that the focus of many of the disciplines is individualistic. And yet I wonder if there might be a place for silence in community. Where we, as believers, come together for the stated purpose of saying nothing but together as members of the body of Christ we come to listen in silence to our head. I have not been able to practice this in a group, although I have for a few moments shared silence with my spiritual director. However, it seems that this has been practiced in some Christian traditions in the past. Take for example what John Woolman recounts in his journal:

> Discouragements and a weight of distress had, at times, attended me in this lonesome walk, but through these afflictions I was mercifully preserved. Sitting down with friends, my mind was turned towards the Lord, to wait for his holy leadings; and in infinite love he was pleased to soften my heart into humble contrition, and renewedly to strengthen me to go forward, so that to me it was a time of heavenly refreshment in a silent meeting.[52]

I wonder if it would not be a profitable exercise to grow in the spiritual discipline of silent listening to the voice of the Lord, if we would arrange times where we would meet with others only for the purpose of entering into the same room as Jesus in absolute stillness? For those of us who are new and learning this practice, it would be both an encouragement and give accountability to meet with others of like mind.

SUSTAINED SILENCE AND SOLITUDE

Small silences and slight solitudes are important as part of everyday life. They help to recentre us and refocus us on what is important. But I have found that sustained periods of time are helpful as well. Many years ago, when I was serving as a pastor the elders allowed me to go on study retreats. I would go to a cabin or take our family camper to a campground and spend two or three days alone. It was before the days of the internet and ubiquitous Wi-Fi. I did not take a radio with me and as a result I lived those hours in silence.

Here is where I would read, pray, sleep, take walks in the woods or by the lake. I would evaluate the past year and plan for the next. Sometimes, God would lead me to study something that even though I didn't know it then, I would need later for my ministry. I look back on those times with fondness. But those study retreats were really mostly for my ministry – and secondarily for my soul.

However, I have explored personal times of solitude. Outside of Nairobi I would often visit the Resurrection Gardens as a place of quiet retreat. The gardens have two main paths with large mosaics depicting the history of salvation up through the life and ministry of Christ. The second path depicts the stations of the cross in large bas relief bronze sculptures ending with the resurrection of Jesus. All throughout the paths the word "Silence!" is both in English and Swahili. There are benches at each mosaic and sculpture where one can sit and meditate on the scene and the accompanying Scriptures.

These times of quiet were valuable in two ways. First, there were times where I felt drawn closer to Jesus as I would sit and listen to him speaking through the Word or through the beauty of the artwork of the grounds. My soul would often become more at rest. I have tried to find these times of solitude in other places as I have gone into forest reserves near where I live now. These are almost always refreshing times.

The second lesson I learned is not to expect too much from my times of solitude. At first, I went with the expectation that God was going to meet me in a spectacular way. I thought I would receive a dramatic insight or some kind of amazing revelation. I never had that happen. At times I might have had some good thoughts or ideas come to me but nothing of the ecstatic experiences I have heard that others have had. As I look back on that I believe that it was too utilitarian. It wasn't relational.

What I have learned is that these times were really to be focused on Jesus and not on me. So, now, I want to come with a sense of expectancy not expectation. What is the difference?

Living with expectations puts God in a box. And it is me wanting God to do what pleases me. But living with expectancy means allowing God to do things the way that please him. Living with expectations means having my hands clenched around what I want. But living with expectancy means having my hands open to receive what God wants to give me. So, if God wants to meet me in an extraordinary way, that is wonderful. If he just wants to meet in a quiet restful way that is wonderful too.

The key point as we draw nearer to Jesus in silence and solitude is that we don't want to insist that our expectations be met. We hold them loosely. Instead, we live in expectancy, and we enter into the adventure with God who may want to do abundantly more than we ask or think. Isaiah writes to the nation of Israel in Isaiah 30:15:

> This is what the Sovereign Lord, the Holy
> One of Israel, says:
> "In repentance and rest is your salvation,
> in quietness and trust is your strength,
> but you would have none of it."

This is a promise for us if we enter into silence and solitude with the Lord. Sadly, the nation did not as Isaiah goes on to say, "but you would have none of it." But Jesus still invites us. "Come to me, all you who are weary and burdened, and I will give you rest" (Matthew 11:28). And the Lord still exhorts us, "Be still, and know that I am God" (Psalm 46:10).

The choice to enter the same room as Jesus and into his presence through the door of silence and solitude is up to each one of us. Will we choose to enter and find rest for our souls?

TURNING THE HANDLE TO THE DOOR OF SILENCE AND SOLITUDE

- Richard Foster writes, "I say we must learn holy listening. We are listening, always listening, for the Divine Whisper amid the human clatter."[53]

  Take some time to reflect on what are extraneous sights and sounds in your life that might be distracting you from entering into the same room with Jesus and hearing his voice and seeing his vision for your life. What are the sources of these distractions?

- What steps could you take to remove or limit these sounds, the human clatter, so that you might be able to hear the still and quiet whisperings of the Spirit of Jesus in your soul?

- What might you do to increase silence and solitude in your life so that you could sit at the feet of Jesus?

- Plan a time for communal silent listening to and meeting with Jesus. Write a list of those who you would like to invite to join with you. Invite them!
- Another way to experience communal silent listening is to attend silent retreats which various communities hold with large groups of participants who might for example, keep silence from the start of the evening until after breakfast as a way to listen for the voice of Jesus.

4

The Door of Awareness

When Jacob awoke from his sleep, he thought, "Surely the Lord is in this place, and I was not aware of it." (Genesis 28:16)

Nothing can take the place of the touch of God in the soul and the sense of Someone there.
– A. W. Tozer[54]

One of my weaknesses is that I can become so focused on what I am doing and what I am interested in that I can become oblivious and unaware of those around me. My wife would have a friend visit and I would walk in the room and not even greet them. My mind was somewhere else so that I might just break in and start talking or asking a question. And then she would give me a glance as she nodded her head in her friend's direction and that would jolt me back to awareness and I would then say, "Hi!" and acknowledge their presence. Now, for the most part, when we have guests, I say hello and enter into a conversation with them.

One of the doors which enters into the same room as Jesus is the door of awareness. I place this chapter following the discussion of silence and solitude because in the world of distraction and noise in which we live it can be quite easy to go through life, day by day, and not be aware of Jesus at all. He is always present but are we conscious of his presence? My wife recently illustrated this when she wrote in our monthly newsletter:

> Katie (our daughter) and her husband Sandy were taking Shiloh for a walk in his stroller. He loves sitting up and looking at the world all around him. The other day he happened to glance up and was surprised to see his mom and dad looking down at him through the screening! How did *they* get there? Of course, they had been there all along. And they had been there *every time* they had taken him out . . . even before he noticed them.

Jesus is always with us; do we acknowledge that he is even around? Does he enter into our thoughts, and do we seek to converse with him? And how do we even do that? It would be so much easier if he was a friend with skin on that we could see and feel and hear and touch. We desire the physical reality of Jesus and thus miss the spiritual reality of his presence. A. W. Tozer puts it this way:

> A spiritual kingdom lies all about us, enclosing us, embracing us, altogether within the reach of our inner selves, waiting for us to recognize it. God himself is here waiting for our response to his presence. The eternal world will come alive to us the moment we begin to reckon upon its reality.[55]

The psalmist seems to be aware of Jesus throughout the day. He asks, "When I remember You on my bed, I meditate on You in the *night* watches" (Psalm 63:6, NKJV). So, for me to become more aware of Jesus I have started saying "Good morning, Jesus!" when I sit down with my Bible early in the morning. Sometimes at night as I go to bed – if I remember and I often don't – I say, "Good night, Jesus!" And I need to do it more during the day. If friendship involves acknowledging the presence of the other, then at least this is a start. This may seem strange and a bit awkward at first, but I have found that as I have consciously addressed Jesus directly throughout the day, it has become easier, and I talk to him more and about more.

For two people to be friends they have to move toward each other. So, I desired to move toward Jesus. As the old saying goes, "If God seems far away, guess who moved?" But Jesus moved toward me when he said, "I chose you" (John 15:16). This is significant and it harkens back to my childhood experience when I was not chosen by others to be on their side in the schoolyard games, or to be their friend. I grew up lonely and longing to belong. As a result, I shut down the relational part of my being to protect myself from further hurt because to belong, to be somebody, to be thought of as significant, has always been a core felt need and a driving motivational force to accomplish and succeed. But then I let these words of Jesus sink deep into my soul, "I have called you friend, I have chosen you." As the reality of these words struck me, I was filled with joy that the Creator of the universe desired me to be on his side. Jesus called "those whom he desired . . . so that they might be with him" (Mark 3:13-14, ESV). What was true of the first disciples, was true of me!

SEEKING JESUS

The process of moving toward Jesus is a process of seeking him. The psalmist says, "I have sought your face with all my heart; be gracious to me according to your promise" (Psalm 119:58). Seeking the face of the Lord is a poetic way of seeking his presence. This was the psalmist's heart's desire. This is the impulse of someone who hungers after God and desires personal intimacy with him. And the psalmist is doing it with all his heart! This is no casual effort. This is an intentional and deliberate searching for a closer relationship. It is done with all of the psalmist's being.

And this searching, within the context of the psalm, this drawing near to intimacy with God – this coming into his presence – is through a wholehearted encounter and engagement with God's word. The psalmist seeks deeper relationship and intimacy through immersion in written revelation. Thus, we have a connection of living out the word in life with seeking God himself. We see this in Psalm 119:2 where the psalmist says, "Blessed are those who keep his statutes and seek him with all their heart." And verse 10, "I seek you with all my heart; do not let me stray from your commands." Straying from the commands of God would hinder the intimacy he is seeking with the Lord.

But this verse also includes a prayer: "Be gracious to me according to your promise." We don't know what the specific scriptural promise was the psalmist had in mind at the time of this writing. Perhaps it was Deuteronomy 30:9b-10:

> The Lord will again delight in you and make you prosperous, just as he delighted in your ancestors, if you obey the Lord your God and keep his commands and decrees that are written in this Book of the Law and turn to the Lord your God with all your heart and with all your soul.

This thought is amplified in Jeremiah 29:13-14a: "'You will seek me and find me when you seek me with all your heart. I will be found by you,' declares the Lord." This is a promise to gladden the heart of the one who is seeking a closer, personal, intimacy with Jesus!

This experience is expressed by Clara Tear Williams who wrote:

All my life long I had a longing
For a drink from some clear spring,
That I hoped would quench the burning
Of the thirst I felt within.

Well of water, ever springing,
Bread of life so rich and free,
Untold wealth that never faileth,
My Redeemer is to me.

Hallelujah! I have found Him
Whom my soul so long has craved!
Jesus satisfies my longings,
Thro' His blood I now am saved.[56]

Cultivating an awareness of being in the presence of Jesus takes time. We have to develop the mental and spiritual habit by training our soul to be thinking of Jesus; of looking for him because he *is present everywhere and always*. C. S. Lewis observes:

> We may ignore, but we can nowhere evade, the presence of God. The world is crowded with him. He walks everywhere *incognito*. And the *incognito* is not always hard to penetrate. The real labour is to remember, to attend. In fact, to become awake. Still more, to remain awake.[57]

I have found that just by talking to God about even little things and asking him to help me with different projects or tasks is helping me to develop sensitivity to his presence. In addition, sentence prayers for myself and others throughout the day keeps me mindful that he is right here with me.

In the book, *The Practice of the Presence of God,* a number of conversations with Brother Lawrence were recorded by an unknown writer. In the second conversation he relates Brother Lawrence's thoughts on developing awareness of God's presence:

> To form a habit of conversing with God continually, and referring all we do to him, we must at first apply to him with some diligence; but that after a little care we should find his love inwardly excite us to it without any difficulty.[58]

May the Lord help us to follow in his footsteps to grow in our awareness of the presence of Jesus and enter into the same room with him. John Baillie prays:

> O Eternal God, although I cannot see you with my eyes or touch you with my hands, give me today a clear conviction of your reality and power. Do not let me go into my work believing only in the world of sense and time, but give me grace to understand that world I cannot see or touch is the most real world of all.[59]

TURNING THE HANDLE TO THE DOOR OF AWARENESS

Turning the handle to help you be more aware of the presence of Jesus can be a matter of prayer. Below are two models that can help you to begin.

- You can use this Puritan writer's prayer to ask the Holy Spirit to increase your awareness of Jesus in your life:

O Holy Spirit, . . .
Vain are all divine purposes of love
and the redemption wrought by Jesus,
except thou work within,
regenerating by thy power,
giving me eyes to see Jesus,
showing me the realities of the unseen
world (emphasis mine).[60]

- Douglas McKelvey in *Every Moment Holy** writes

For you, O Lord, are with us always.
Every sphere of life and creation is Yours,
and all are threads of the same bright weave:
our goings-out and our comings-in,
our fellowship and our loneliness,
our youth and our old age,
our passions and our vocations,
our chores and our entertainments. You are
equally present in our failures and
in our successes,
in our sleep and in our wakeful hours,
in our tears and in our laughter,
in our births, in our lives,
and even in the hour of our deaths . . .
train the hearts of your people to practice
a mindfulness of your presence
in all moments.[61]

---

* *Every Moment Holy* is a collection of 111 liturgies and prayers for every moment of life from the mundane to the profound and eternal which help the reader to live out each experience of life in the awareness of their sacredness in the presence of Jesus. Some examples include: "The Ritual of Morning Coffee," "For Changing Diapers." "For Leaving on a Holiday," "For those Facing the Loss of Memory," "For the Anniversary of a Loss," and "A Liturgy for Dying Well."

- In light of this, use this prayer of Andrew Murray to pray for an increasing mindfulness of the presence of Jesus. He writes: "Enter into the holy presence and plead with God, praying, 'Oh, that I might have the blessing of knowing that Jesus is with me at every moment and forever.'"[62]

- Whenever my son sees that the time on our digital clock is 3:16, he says "It is Jesus's time." Think of other ways for you that would be tangible reminders to be aware of Jesus. It could be certain songs, artwork, or even a delightful alarm tone on your watch or phone that would occasionally ring to help you develop of being aware of Jesus.

- One way of cultivating a deeper awareness of the presence of Jesus is to intentionally enter into a time of solitude and silence as discussed in chapter 3. Plan a time to practice this discipline and in quiet and free from distractions, open your heart to an awareness of his presence.

5

The Door of Beauty

A landscape can sing about God.
– Dag Hammarskjöld[63]

Along our way, in such places
whose contours you deliberately created,
may we pause to savour the evidences
of your diverse imagination
expressed in glories of scenery . . .
rouse also our hearts
that we might be quietly shaped
by those whisperings of divine beauty.
– Douglas Kaine McKelvey[64]

Beauty is something that is newly being opened to me. I believe in my younger days I was too insecure to enter into the beauty around me. Since I had shut down a lot of my emotional side I had no capacity or ability to appreciate it, or at least acknowledge it. It didn't fit the *macho* image (shell?) I wanted to project. I was a *man* forgetting that I was *human* made in the image of the creator of beauty and all that is lovely.

So, I am learning. I am learning to see beauty in the everyday things of life. And my wife is my guide. She sees beauty in the subtle or bold colours of the clouds and the delicate flowers of the chickweed. She is thrilled with the splendour of the farming landscapes of Lancaster County. She exults in the riot of colours displayed in the drying clothes stretched out on the line between house and barn. She finds beauty in the fragrance of the lilac and lily of the valley growing outside our door. Music moves her and she thrills to the glory of God reflected in the anatomy of the human body. And these displays of beauty often are met with expressions of thanks and praise to God.

C. S. Lewis describes the same joy in worship in nature as he describes a brook and a small waterfall. He writes:

> That cushiony moss, that coldness and sound and dancing light were no doubt very minor blessings compared with 'the means of grace and the hope of glory'. But then they were manifest. So far as they were concerned, sight had replaced faith. They were not the hope of glory, they were an exposition of the glory itself . . . I have tried, since that moment, to make every pleasure into a channel of adoration.[65]

As we open the door of beauty, these declarations of worship take us into the same room as Jesus – into his presence. Thomas Merton writes, "We ought to be alive enough to reality to see beauty all around us. Beauty is simply reality itself, perceived in a special way that gives it a resplendent value of its own."[66] And God is reality himself. Thus, beauty in the world is a form of revelation of God himself. Or as one of my pastor friends said recently, "We need to see the glory of God reflected in the beauty of nature." Thus, beauty should move us toward God. Beauty is a gateway to worship and worship is the key that opens the door of our heart to intimacy with Jesus who is the creator of beauty.

Again, quoting Merton, "One of the most important – and most neglected elements in the beginning of the interior life is the ability to *respond* to reality, to see the value and the beauty in ordinary things, to come alive to the splendour that is all around us in the creatures of God" (emphasis mine).[67]

We do not worship the creation, but we revel in the reality of the creator that is reflected in creation's beauty. Augustine views this physical and tangible enjoying of the beauty of created things as only an outward symbol of an inner spiritual and relational encounter with God. He writes:

> But what is it that I love in loving thee? Not physical beauty, nor the splendour of time, nor the radiance of the light – so pleasant to our eyes – nor the sweet melodies of the various kinds of songs, nor the fragrant smell of flowers and ointments and spices; not manna and honey, not the limbs embraced in physical love – it is not these I love when I love my God. Yet it is true that I love a certain kind of light and sound and fragrance and food and embrace in loving my God, who is the light and sound and fragrance and food and embracement of my inner man – where that light shines into my soul which no place can contain, where time does not snatch away the lovely sound, where no breeze disperses the sweet fragrance, where no eating diminishes the food there provided, and where there is an embrace that no satiety comes to sunder. This is what I love when I love my God.[68]

Each experience and acknowledgement of beauty is an opportunity to think of Jesus and to thank and worship him as the creator. This then can increase our relationship and friendship with him because we are engaging with him on the level of reality. He is the creator of our reality because he is reality himself. Thus, as creatures we can enter into a fellowship and friendship and intimacy with Jesus through communion in the reality of beauty. John Baillie in his classic work, *A Diary of Private Prayer* captures this so clearly in his prayer:

> Creator Spirit, who forever hovers over the lands and waters of earth, enriching them with forms and colours that no human skill can copy, give me today the mind and heart to rejoice in your creation.
>
> Forbid that I should walk through your beautiful world with unseeing eyes. . . .
>
> Let the energy and vigour which in your wisdom you have infused into every living thing stir within my being today, so that I may not be a lazy or mindless bystander among your creatures; . . .
>
> And above all give me grace to use these beauties of earth around me and this eager stirring of life within me to lift my soul from creature to Creator, and from nature to nature's God.[69]

So, we need to be aware, but we must also be careful not to analyse at the moment. This destroys the wonder of the worship experience. Think of trying to go to an orchestra concert with beautiful and majestic music filling the auditorium and you are sitting there and wondering what the meter is and why the piece is in the key of C major instead of E major and why the trombone is playing the bass line instead of the tuba.

These are valid inquiries but would distract from entering into the emotional delight of what we are hearing. So we should sit back and listen and revel in the end for which it was created. As C. S. Lewis says, "The great work of art was made for the sake of all it does and is, down to the curve of every wave and the flight of every insect."[70] And so we should just enjoy beauty in nature, art, words, or in any form, and give praise to the Creator who, when he finished his work, pronounced it very good (see Genesis 1:31).

One of the ways we enjoy beauty is to share it with others, especially people that we love. This is why we may point out to our spouse, children, or friends, the colours of the sky, the amazing cloud formations, the sparkling of the morning dew diamonds on the grass, the iridescence of a bird's wing. This sharing enhances our enjoyment and bonds us together in the experience. So, as I have developed my relational relationship with Jesus, I take delight in drawing attention to the beauty in his creation and we bond together in the experience. I enter again into the same room with him.

And thus, I enter into the presence of the source of beauty. For where does beauty come from? In a stanza of the hymn "Fairest Lord Jesus" that is often omitted in hymn books we are given the source. It is the beauty of Jesus:

> All fairest beauty, heavenly and earthly,
> Wondrously, Jesus, is found in Thee;
> None can be nearer, fairer or dearer,
> Than Thou, my Saviour, art to me.[71]

Notice how the psalmist draws out the connection between beauty and the presence of the Lord. In Psalm 27:4 the psalmist writes, "One thing I have asked from the Lord, that I shall seek: That I may dwell in the house of the Lord all the days of my life, to behold the beauty of the Lord and to meditate in His temple" (NASB). As the psalmist came into the presence of the Lord in his temple, he came to behold the beauty of the Lord.

The Hebrew word translated *beauty* in Psalm 27:4 is literally defined as *delightfulness*.[72] As we take delight in the beauty of our creator's handiwork it is a wonderful reflection of what our souls can experience when we enter into the same room as Jesus, and we delight in the beauty of his presence.

John Baillie, summarizes the thoughts of this chapter when he writes:

> Open my eyes, O God, so that I may see you in your wonderful creation around me. Let all lovely things fill my heart with joy, and may they turn my mind to your everlasting loveliness. Forgive me for the times when I have been blind to the grandeur and glory of creation, the charm of little children, and the beauty of human lives, *and so have failed to see you in all these reminders of your presence* (emphasis mine).[73]

TURNING THE HANDLE TO THE DOOR OF BEAUTY

- What is beautiful for you? Is it art, a poem, a piece of music, a little baby, the wonders of nature? Do you enjoy it for the beauty itself? Or do you allow it to be a door that opens your heart to worship Jesus, the Creator?
- As with other disciplines, cultivating the habit of drawing near to Jesus through beauty takes time and effort at first. Every day begin to consciously look for what is beautiful in big and little ways. As you see them, whether in the delicate wings of a butterfly, or the cloud formations in a bright blue sky, or the soft fragrance of garden flowers, make a point to share it with someone by inviting them in the spirit of Psalm 66:5, "Come and see the works of God" (NKJV). This intention to share beauty with someone else will encourage us to worship and draw near to Jesus through the door of beauty.

6

The Door of Commonality

Friends have all things in common.
– Plato[74]

There can be no closeness of relationship if there is no commonality. Commonality means to share features or characteristics. It is more than just having something in common or the same interests, although that is part of it. So, if commonality is a door into the same room as Jesus we must ask, "What can a creature have in common with a transcendent God?" One way is for our spirits to meet or enter into an appreciation and an awareness of his attributes and his beauty. So as Jesus lived out these attributes in the flesh, perhaps I can relate to Jesus and draw near to him by seeking to live them out in my relationship with him as I become more like him and conformed to his likeness in my character and behaviour.

The obvious conclusion to all of this seems to be that if I am going to have a closeness to Jesus, we must have things in common. To put it more personally and intimately: If I am going to have a close relationship with him, I must be interested in the things that interest Jesus and enter into them so that we can experience them together.

This raises the question, "What things is Jesus interested in?" Which leads to another important question, "Am I interested in the things of Jesus?" But a close relationship goes two ways, and so I must also ask myself the convicting question, "Is Jesus interested in my things?" If the answer to the last question is *no*, then I must evaluate my own heart and ask myself, "Do I want intimacy with Jesus enough to give up those things he is not interested in?"

It seems that the criterion by which to evaluate my things would be the attributes of God. Thus, if I cannot with integrity relate my things to one or more of God's attributes, then that specific thing or activity is not something that I could build an intimate relationship with Jesus upon.

In application to my daily life and activities, I then must ask what do Jesus and I have in common in this activity? Or what am I able to find in common with Jesus in this activity or experience? What can I share with Jesus in what I do and or experience? What can I share with Jesus in what I perceive he is doing?

After I came to the place where I wanted to share the experiences of my life in common with Jesus, I put this to the test. My first experience of daily life was to go to the dentist to get my permanent crown installed. As I sat in the dentist chair, I asked Jesus about which of his attributes he was expressing here. Whatever it was, I wanted to share. I knew intellectually he was with me in the room, but I was not feeling anything. I tried to conjure up something like being amazed at the skill of the dentist and the technology that he was employing as he ground down both my opposing molar and the crown to make a perfect bite. But I was not feeling it. Then while I waited for the cement to dry, I looked out the window and there in the barren bush in the lot next door appeared a gorgeous cardinal. And Jesus and I smiled together. I felt it now.

As I reflected on this later, the lyrics from a song by the ska[75] musical group the Supertones came to my mind which talked about the care Jesus has for us. It says, "When I'm in a dentist's chair it matters, it matters." Jesus and I shared a good laugh on that one. Imagine Jesus enjoying ska! And then tears filled my eyes as I felt Jesus was sitting next to me. Richard Foster writes:

> To believe that God can reach us and bless us in the ordinary junctures of daily life is the stuff of prayer. But we want to throw this away, so hard is it for us to believe that God would enter our space . . . Do you remember Moses at the burning bush? God had to tell him to take off his shoes – he did not know he was on holy ground. And if we can just come to see that right where we are is holy ground – in our jobs and homes, with our co-workers and friends and families. This is where we learn to pray.[76]

Speaking of the ordinary junctures of life, which is focused on sharing experiences with Jesus, it seems to me that the common and mundane activities must be examined in this light as well. Too often the mistake is made that living life with Jesus must be made on the Mount of Transfiguration level. These experiences may come from time to time, but even Jesus didn't stay on the mountain top. He descended into the valley of real life soon after his glorifying experience. Thus, sharing life with Jesus must extend to the common details of everyday life.

Andrew Peterson captures the essence of these thoughts in the foreword of *Every Moment Holy*, when he writes about our duty to reclaim and remember the sacredness of our lives and life itself. He says:

> By remembering the holiness of each moment, we banish the old Gnostic ghost and thwart its lie that there's nothing holy about flesh and bone, soil and stone, work and pleasure, and all tangible, tactile,

> visible things. The resurrection of Jesus sent shockwaves into every molecule of creation, even into this crazy century of ones and zeroes and jet engines. If the gospel is true, then it matters in all of time and space – from a thousand years ago at the Norman conquest of England to ten minutes ago when I ate a cookie; it matters from the moons of Jupiter to the couch where I am writing this . . . The gospel matters even here. Even now.[77]

When we change our perspective to believe and live every moment holy in the presence of Jesus it can have a transforming effect in our lives. This is because the transformation of ordinary life into sacred life is the foundation for a deeper and more mature relationship with Jesus.

Let me give an example which is mundane and may even seem silly. However, I cannot escape it because I am committed to share everything in my life with Jesus. From time to time my wife will travel for two or three weeks either on ministry or family matters. For years I have lived those weeks when she is away as I suspect many men do. I wait two or three days to do the dishes. I don't make the bed because in twelve hours I will just get back under the covers. And I don't sweep or vacuum until the day before my wife gets back. Why? Because I was living alone.

But now that I am seeking to live every experience, and every act of my life in common with Jesus, the thought came to me that Jesus would want the bed made. If God is a God of order then Jesus desires order and cleanliness and neatness. The truth is that when my wife is away from home, I am not living alone. I am sharing the house with Jesus. And logically, he does not prefer to live in a messy home. So now with Jesus, I make the bed, wash the dishes, tidy up around the house, and wash the car.

This is not new. Brother Lawrence, that godly monastery cook of the 1300s said:

> We can do little things for God. I turn the cake that is frying on the pan for love of him, and that done, if there is nothing else to call me, I prostrate myself in worship before him, who has given me grace to work; afterwards I rise happier than a king. It is enough for me to pick up but a straw from the ground for the love of God.[78]

Brother Lawrence talks about little things. But, in fact, in comparison with an infinite God all the things we do are little things. So, no matter what God calls us to do with our lives, we should do them for the love of God and do them in companionship with Jesus. Thus, doing the dishes, making the bed, sweeping the floor, or washing the car are not compartmentalized as time-consuming chores but are changed into times spent with Jesus. Looking at it this way it gives a whole new meaning to redeeming the time! As the Puritan wrote, "Give me a holy avarice to redeem the time."[79]

The principle of commonality should also be applied in the areas of our activities and entertainment. We need to ask would I be able to ask Jesus to participate with me in this activity? Would I be able to listen to this song along with Jesus? Would I be comfortable in asking Jesus to watch certain television shows or movies? When I surf the internet and scroll through various pages on my phone, would Jesus be comfortable with my choice of "clicks"? This is a simple way to evaluate our leisure time and the things we participate in. If we can't share them with Jesus, then we will not be sitting in the same room with him. Our fellowship will be broken.

However, experiencing commonality with Jesus in the little things and tasks of life, and in our leisure activities, extends to our acts of our life's work as well. Perhaps it goes without saying, but we should be examining what we are doing in the area of our service and ministry. In what we are doing to serve the Lord, would Jesus be comfortable with how we were serving him? Would he be pleased with our attitudes, actions, motives, methods, and how we treat our fellow workers, etc.? Could he participate fully with us, or would there be little commonality between his way of working and ours?

If Jesus would not be able to participate with us in our service for him, then in spite of all our efforts he will be far away. And our service will not be bearing fruit for eternity. This is what Jesus said in John 15:4-5:

> Remain in me, as I also remain in you. No branch can bear fruit by itself; it must remain in the vine. Neither can you bear fruit unless you remain in me. I am the vine; you are the branches. If you remain in me and I in you, you will bear much fruit; apart from me you can do nothing.

We would do well to evaluate our service for the Lord. We can start with the Puritan's prayer, "Permit me not to labour at work which thou wilt not bless."[80]

As we close this chapter on commonality with Jesus, we see that asking the simple questions "Can I share this with Jesus, and would he be able to share this with me?" can be a powerful way to live in fellowship with Jesus and to remain in the same room as him.

TURNING THE HANDLE TO THE DOOR OF COMMONALITY

- Evaluate how would it affect your choice of reading or viewing and listening to various media such as television, movies, music, podcasts, and audiobooks, etc., if you were to invite Jesus to share the experience with you? If you are willing to do that, pray this prayer by John Baillie:

> O God, give me today a strong and vivid sense that you are by my side. In a crowd or by myself, in business and leisure, in my sitting down and my rising, may I always be aware of your presence beside me. By your grace, O God, I will go nowhere today where you cannot come, nor seek anyone's presence that would rob me of yours. By your grace I will let no thought enter my heart that might hinder my closeness with you, nor let any word come from my mouth that is not meant for your ear. So shall my courage be firm and my heart be at peace . . . Amen.[81]

- Evaluate how it would change your attitude and how you would go about your work, chores, and other responsibilities if you talked with Jesus about them and as you completed them.
- As you serve Jesus, how would it affect your motives, your methods, and your manner if you would evaluate it in light of his presence and in the awareness of every moment holy? How would it affect you if he would be able to participate in your ministry and the way you are conducting it?

7

The Door of Scripture

If I oppose the Word,
I oppose my Lord
when he is near.
If I receive the Word,
I receive my Lord
wherein he is nigh.
– Arthur Bennett[82]

"Read your Bible; pray every day and you'll grow, grow, grow!"[83] So go the words of a song I sang in Sunday School classes, Vacation Bible School, and Youth Group. So early on in my Christian experience it was ingrained in my being that this is what a believer did. In fact, as I started this journey into the same room as Jesus, I hadn't even thought of the door of Scripture. Being in the Word everyday has been a life-habit. It was so obvious, that I didn't think that it needed to be included. But then, is it so obvious?

When I was doing a seminar for about 400 pastors and church leaders in Kenya I was speaking on the pastor's spiritual life. When I asked for a show of hands of those who had a daily time in the Word and in prayer only 10 per cent of them indicated that they did. I wonder if this was true for these pastors, what would be the experience of the members of their congregations?

Of course, in Africa and other places in the world, being in the Word daily may not be possible, as many may not even have the Scriptures available in their own language or they may be too poor to even own their own Bible. This is sad and we should seek to find ways to address this challenge, but it is beyond the scope of this book to do so.

Much has been written about the importance of being in the Scripture on a regular basis, so I won't repeat that here. However, I do believe that this practice is an important doorway into the same room as Jesus and in entering into a dialogue with him. As the saying goes, "We speak to him in prayer; he speaks to us in the Word." Richard Foster affirms this when he writes:

> We must first have our minds filled with and disciplined by Scripture before we can, with genuine profit, enter into the presence of the Holy in unmediated communion. We are to emulate the faithful described in the Psalm . . . whose "delight is in the law of the Lord, and on his law they meditate day and night" (Ps. 1:2).[84]

Let me give you an example from my own life which can be helpful for those of us who are not consistent in our time in the Word and thus not entering into the dialogue with Jesus. When I was a young pastor, I had a difficult time in being consistent in my quiet time. I was so busy, I had a family, and so often I would just skip my time in the Word and in prayer.

Then I attended a conference where the speaker challenged us to make a solemn vow to the Lord to read the Bible for a least five minutes a day. He said that it didn't sound like much, but it would help us to be consistent. He said, "Don't promise an hour or even a half an hour. Because you won't be able to keep that vow. It is too big. You can do more than you vow. Promise just five minutes as that is a vow you can keep." So, I did.

At first it was hard, and I would forget, and after a long day I would get into bed and the Holy Spirit would whisper, "You didn't read your Bible today!" And so, I would get up, grab my Bible, and read for five minutes and then go back to bed. Do you think I got too much out of my reading on those nights? No. But it helped me to become consistent. The times that I have missed have been when I have been traveling or been sick or my routine has been totally interrupted. And I can say that in the 40 or so years since I made that vow there are very few days when I haven't read my Bible.

Richard Foster, in describing the practice of reading Scripture and its value in the Christian walk, writes:

> When reading the Bible, people commonly experience a special "word in the Word," in which a particular passage seems to apply to an individual situation in a new way. Sometimes I wonder if in such experiences God is working through the creative factor of the brain to bring to the conscious mind wonderful new combinations of ideas and insights. At any rate, this "quickening of the Word" encourages us that *God is near* and deeply interested in the particular experiences of our lives (emphasis mine).[85]

It is important to understand that not every day, or with every passage of Scripture that we may read will we feel the presence of Jesus. Some claim that we can see Jesus in every verse of Scripture. However, it may be a lack of spiritual insight on my part, but I don't feel close to Jesus reading the genealogies of 1 Chronicles, or the woe pronounced on Edom for their pride in the prophecy of Obadiah, or the perversity of the Benjaminites of Gibeah. These are instructive, but they do nothing to increase my desire for intimacy with Jesus.

Dr. Walter Kaiser, President Emeritus of Gordon-Conwell Theological Seminary, says that it is "impossible to lay the claim that our Lord Jesus must be found in every text of Scripture; indeed, on every one of its pages."[86] So, we shouldn't feel that something is wrong if we don't feel like we are entering into the same room as Jesus when we read some passages of Scripture.

However, having said this, the more we engage in the discipline of reading God's Word the more we will become aware of his presence and his desire to communicate with us. Our receptivity to his voice will continue to grow as we see in the following description by A. W. Tozer:

> I think for the average person the progression will be something like this: First, a sound as of a Presence walking in the garden. Then a voice, more intelligible, but still far from clear. Then the happy moment when the Spirit begins to illuminate the Scriptures, and that which had been only a sound, or at best a voice, now becomes an intelligible word, warm and intimate and clear as the word of a dear friend. Then will come life and light, and best of all, ability to see and rest in and embrace Jesus Christ as Saviour and Lord and All.[87]

Let me close this chapter with one final caution. This is primarily for those of us who are pastors or teachers of the Word. This is the temptation that when we are seeking to feed our souls with Scripture, we can easily turn our time into sermon or lesson preparation for others and how we will apply it to them.

I talked to my spiritual director about this, and he said, "Those of us with the calling to share the Word with others have this unique challenge. Sometimes, I wish I could just study the Word and practice the disciplines in anonymity and without anyone knowing it." Richard Foster acknowledges the same concern when he says:

> Whereas the study of Scripture centres on exegesis, the meditation upon Scripture centres on internalizing and personalizing the passage. The written Word becomes a living word addressed to us. This is time not for technical studies or analysis or even the gathering of material to share with others.[88]

What should we do if this is our case? First, be aware of the temptation. Ask the Spirit to teach you and to guide you into the truth of the passage for you personally. Finally, if you start to drift off into preparation mode, call yourself back to personal application mode. But don't be too angry or harsh with yourself. Instead hold up your hands in a mode of receptivity and as an expression of invitation and say, "Father, help me to receive this truth for myself and my life first." It is through this that we will not preach or teach theoretically or unrealistically beyond our experience if the time comes when we will be led to share what we have learned. This takes discipline, but it is possible when we are intentionally turning away from our professional approach and instead, like Mary in Luke 10:39, sit at the feet of Jesus and learn in his presence.

TURNING THE HANDLE TO THE DOOR OF SCRIPTURE

- In this chapter, the author described his experience and making a vow to the Lord. Do you desire to be more consistent in hearing the voice of Jesus through reading Scripture? If so, would you be willing to promise the Lord, that you will read the Bible for at least 5 minutes a day?

Remember, you can do more. It will help you to become more consistent! The Holy Spirit will remind you of your vow if you forget.

However, only make this commitment if you are serious about entering into a deeper and more intimate relationship by entering through Scripture into the same room as Jesus.

8

The Door of Prayer

This is to ask for what I desire. Here it will be
to ask for an intimate knowledge of our Lord
who has become man for me, that I may
love him more and follow him more closely.
– Ignatius of Loyola[89]

The story is told of the little boy who was afraid of the dark and had trouble falling asleep. So, he would call his father and ask him to stay with him. The father tried to comfort him and said, "You don't have to be afraid because God is with you right here in your room." To which his son, replied, "I can't see him. I want a God with skin on."

I know that I have echoed his desire in my own heart. And when it comes to prayer, that is my desire even more. We are often told that prayer is just having a conversation with God. But I struggle with that because my conversation seems to be one way. I talk, but I don't hear anybody immediately responding. I want a God with skin on. Well, who is God with skin on? It is Jesus, and I don't want him by himself in the next room.

So, in my prayer life I often address God as Father. This is the example of Jesus in the Lord's Prayer as he began his prayer, "Our Father in heaven" (Matthew 6:9). But he is also our King and even though we are told to come with confidence (NIV) or boldly (NKJV), to the throne of grace, it is still a throne, nonetheless (Hebrews 4:16). Thus, there is no place for a flippant or casual manner. Jesus is our friend and brother, but he is also our glorious king! We would do well to remember Foster's counsel: "The intimacy of prayer must be always counterbalanced by the infinite distance of creature to Creator."[90]

However, realizing the importance of our manner of approach and coming into the presence of God and the precious privilege of encountering God personally, prayer is a primary way of engaging with the King and Creator of the universe. Tim Keller puts it this way:

> Conversation with God leads to an encounter with God . . . Prayer turns theology into experience. Through it *we sense his presence* and receive his joy, his love, his peace, and confidence, and thereby we are changed in attitude, behaviour, and character (emphasis mine).[91]

Part of moving into the same room with Jesus through the door of prayer is to come in just as we are. God knows us anyway. And he knows us personally as David says:

> O Lord, You have searched me and known me.
> You know when I sit down and when I get up;
> You understand my thought from far away.
> You scrutinize my path and my lying down,
> And are *acquainted with all my ways*
> (Psalm 139:1-3, NASB, emphasis mine).

God created us as special and unique one-of-a-kind persons. And so he wants to have fellowship with us in our own one-of-a-kind way. This is because he delights in us just as we are. Thus, we can have true intimacy when we humbly accept this truth. This is because Jesus wants to have a relationship with the real us and not with some self-serving prideful image which we have created or are trying to project.* As C. S. Lewis says, "The prayer preceding all prayers is, 'May it be the real I who speaks. May it be the real Thou I speak to.'"[92]

John Woolman was a man who prayed without ceasing as he sought to know the will of God and to rely on him for guidance and strength to do his will. On one occasion when he had agreed to go to minister, he describes his concerns and his dependence upon God:

> After I had given up to go, the thoughts of the journey were often attended with unusual sadness; in which times my heart was frequently turned to the Lord with inward breathings for his heavenly support, that I might not fail to follow him wheresoever he might lead me.[93]

Thomas Merton writes, "The most important thing in prayer is that we present ourselves as we are before God as he is . . . Our sincerity itself establishes an instant contact with the God of all truth."[94]

How do we establish this instant contact with God? And then carry that contact on into conversation in his presence? This starts with living in awareness of him as we discussed in chapter 4 about the door of awareness. Awareness of what God is saying to us in the beauty of creation and throughout all of life should lead us to follow the urging of the psalmist who says, "Talk of all His wondrous works" (Psalm 105:2, NKJV).

---

* While we are speaking of private prayer, this also speaks to the prideful temptation to project a certain image in public prayer as well. If I am trying to appear spiritual in public prayer, then to whom am I really praying?

As we do this our thoughts will be focused on the God who is present with us in all of his indescribable essence and thus in fearful awe, we will realize who it is that welcomes us into the glory of his presence. As Austin Phelps writes:

> God is here, within these walls; before me, behind me, on my right hand, on my left hand. He who fills immensity has come down to me here. I am now about to bow at his feet, and *speak* to him . . . I may pour forth my desires before him, and not one syllable from my lips shall escape his ear. I may speak to him as I would to the dearest friend I have on earth.[95]

TURNING THE HANDLE TO THE DOOR OF PRAYER

- If you are struggling with prayer you can come to Jesus and ask for his help to grow in your prayer life. You could use this prayer as a model:

  > Oh Jesus, I am like the disciples who observed your prayer life and communion with the Father. In the Lord's Prayer (Matthew 6:9-13) you taught us how to pray. But the disciples requested "Teach us to pray" (Luke 11:1). And so today I am asking you to teach me to pray and teach me how so that I may enter more deeply into your presence and abide with you. Amen.

- Paul says, "Pray continually" in 1 Thessalonians 5:17. This has been described as maintaining an attitude of prayer, but I believe it can be, and should be more than attitude – it should be action. Begin to develop the practice of taking everything to the Lord in prayer. Begin to just say short sentence prayers when you see people, hear about situations, face a difficulty at work, or are confronted with a difficult relationship encounter. For example, in the morning, I often whisper a prayer for my neighbours as I watch them go to work from my office window. My wife and I will pray after we get an email or a text message from a friend, or when we hear of someone who is sick or who has been bereaved.

  These prayers do not take a lot of time, but they keep us near to Jesus as we bring these people and their needs to him. May I encourage you to begin this practice and stay in the same room as Jesus throughout the day.

9

The Door of Confession

In confession the light of the Gospel breaks into the darkness and the seclusion of the heart.
– Dietrich Bonhoeffer[96]

"I have a good memory, but it's short" was the joke that one of the leaders in my congregation would often make. And while we may smile about that as it applies to everyday events, and people's names and faces, it is a serious thing when it comes to the specific sins that we commit daily. This is because our sins break the fellowship we have with Jesus and makes living in his presence impossible. Speaking of this, the Puritan writes, "My great evil is that I do not remember the sins of my youth, nay, the sins of one day I forget the next."[97] I identify with this saying completely and have included it in my phone prayer app, using it as a reminder to ask the Holy Spirit to help me remember my sins. And not too long ago as I was praying this prayer, the Holy Spirit answered.

He brought to my mind an incident which happened almost ten years ago where I had written something in an evaluation that was harsh and critical out of jealousy for the person's success. This was not the first time the Spirit had reminded me of what I had done, but each time I rationalized my action because they had asked for my opinion and besides it was anonymous. But now I was willing to confess it and to ask for forgiveness.

As I was sharing with my brother about why I was calling and that in the past I had made, but not always followed, a commitment to confession, he said, "I am glad to hear that. We don't hear too much about confession these days." He then graciously forgave me, and our relationship was restored.

Sin in our lives is an absolute block to intimacy with Jesus. We see this truth in the prophet Isaiah's words, "But your iniquities have *separated* you from your God; your *sins* have hidden his face from you, so that he will not hear" (Isaiah 59:2, emphasis mine). Thus, we see that unconfessed sin will keep us from entering into the same room as Jesus. This was the experience of the psalmist who said: "If I had not confessed the sin in my heart, the Lord would not have listened" (Psalm 66:18, NLT).

But what is confession? In 1 John 1:9 we read that, "If we confess our sins, he is faithful and just and will forgive us our sins and purify us from all unrighteousness." The Greek word for confess is *homologeo* which means to say the same thing. When we confess our sins, we are saying the same thing about them that God does. In fact, as C. S. Lewis says, "To confess our sins before God is certainly to tell him what he knows much better than we."[98] There is no belittling what we have done, no excuses or rationalizations, and no making it sound better than it really is: a violation of God's standard of righteousness.

In Luke 7 we have the story of the sinful woman who came into the same room as Jesus. He was reclining at dinner which meant that while facing inward towards the table his feet were pointing outward. And there, at his feet she stood behind him weeping and wetting his feet with her tears, wiping them with her hair and then kissing them and anointing them with perfume. We have no actual words of confession from this woman, but her actions were those of a contrite woman seeking forgiveness for her sin.

And as she sought forgiveness, her confession by action, brought her into the very presence of Jesus and she shared a deeply personal connection with him. And Jesus said, "I tell you her many sins have been forgiven – for she loved much!" And as she loved much, she received much love from Jesus who forgave her of her sins.

Confession leads to forgiveness. And when we are forgiven, we can enter into fellowship with our Saviour. The poet George Herbert speaks of this in his poem "Love" where Jesus is talking with one of his children. Let me share an excerpt here:

> Love bade me welcome: yet my soul drew back
> Guilty of dust and sin . . .
>
> [The reluctant child responds to the invitation.]
>
> . . . let my shame
> Go where it doth deserve.
>
> And know you not, says Love, who bore the blame?
> My dear, then I will serve.
> You must sit down, says Love, and taste my meat:
> So I did sit and eat.[99]

This loving forgiveness in response to our prayer of confession is an expression of the loving heart of our God, our Saviour, our brother, our friend, our Jesus! Dietrich Bonhoeffer affirms that confession opens the door to the same room as Jesus when he says:

> In confession the break-through to new life occurs. Where sin is hated, admitted, and forgiven, there the break with the past is made. "Old things are passed away." But where there is a break with sin, there is conversion . . . "Behold, all things are

> become new" (2 Cor. 5:17). Christ has made a new beginning with us.[100]

Thus, this new beginning can be a renewed and fresh fellowship with Jesus. The Puritan captures this thought in his prayer:

> Thou hast made known to me
> that to save me is Christ's work
> but to *cleave to him* by faith is my work,
> and with this faith is the necessity of my
> daily repentance
> as a mourning for the sin which grace has
> removed . . .
> so that I may live always near the cross
> (emphasis mine).[101]

And may I add, and so that I may live always in the presence of Jesus!

Perhaps, however, there is no clearer illustration of the door of confession than that of the prodigal son seen in Luke 15. The one who left his father's presence, wasted his inheritance in sinful living, and ended up in a such a desperate condition that he desires to eat the food of the pigs he is tending. There he repents, returns to his father, admits his sin, and is received back into fellowship with his father. The door of confession swings wide open as contrition leads to confession. Confession leads to forgiveness. Forgiveness leads to restoration of presence in the same room as Jesus.

However, there are times when we may confess something to the Lord and yet not feel forgiven. For me this has been the case when I remember sins of my youth when there is no way to go back and confess personally and make restitution. They were secret sins where no one knew about them or were foolish things that I did which could have harmed others or were illegal and where I was never caught. The same sins kept coming back to haunt my mind and conscience. I had confessed and asked for forgiveness periodically over the years. Why don't I get full release?

As I wrestled with this lack of feeling forgiveness over specific sinful actions in my life that no one but God knew, I explored the whole idea of what is confession to a brother and what it would look like in my own life. James 5:16 instructs this action when the apostle writes, "Therefore confess your sins to each other and pray for each other so that you may be healed." Some limit this healing to physical healing as is discussed in verse 15, but it seems that James is moving from the specific of physical healing to the more general thought of spiritual healing. This is because we are to confess our sin to one another and not the elders as in the previous verse. Also, the word *healed* is used for deliverance from other ills of many kinds and from sin and its consequences (Matthew 13:15, John 12:40, Hebrews 12:13).[102]

This is a command which I believe is often neglected and yet, it is a necessary action of obedience which can help us to be released from the grip of hidden and secret sins and find healing for our souls. When following this command to confess to a brother or sister, we will find that it brings relief and freedom from the past shame and guilt of our sin. Sin loses its power, and Satan loses his leverage in our souls, when through confession to a trusted friend we bring the sin to light. Then they can affirm our forgiveness in the name of Jesus based on the promises of Scripture that he "forgives all [our] sins" (Psalm 103:3).

We who are from a Protestant background may struggle with this idea of confession to another person whom we have not sinned against and who can forgive those sins. To help us understand this I want to share a lengthy quote from Dietrich Bonhoeffer* which explains this biblical truth. He writes:

* I would encourage the reader to read in its entirety, chapter V "Confession and Communion," in Bonhoeffer's *Life Together* as he lays out the rationale for confession of our sins to a trusted brother or sister in Christ.

> Christ became our Brother in the flesh in order that we might believe in him. In him the love of God came to the sinner. Through him [people] could be sinners and only so could they be helped. All sham was ended in the presence of Christ. The misery of the sinner and the mercy of God – this was the truth of the Gospel in Jesus Christ. It was in this truth that his church was to live. Therefore, he gave his followers the authority to hear the confession of sin and to forgive sin in his name. "Whose soever (sic) sins ye remit, they are remitted unto them: and whose soever (sic) sins ye retain, they are retained" (John 20:23).
>
> When he did that Christ made the church, and in it our brother [or sister], a blessing to us. Now our [fellow believer] stands in Christ's stead. Before [my fellow believer] I need no longer to dissemble. Before him [or her] alone in the whole world I dare to be the sinner that I am; here the truth of Jesus Christ and his mercy rules. Christ became our Brother in order to help us. Through him our [fellow believer] has become Christ for us in the power and authority of the commission Christ has given to him [or her]. Our [fellow believer] stands before us as the sign of the truth and the grace of God. He [or she] has been given to us to help us. He [or she] hears the confession of our sins in Christ's stead and . . . forgives our sins in Christ's name.[103]

As I did this research, and in discussion with my spiritual director, I came to the point where I believed I needed to confess these sins to another person who stood in the place of Christ to me. As a result, I confessed those haunting sins of my youth – some committed forty or more years in the past – and he pronounced forgiveness of those sins in Jesus's name based on the shed blood of Christ for their remission. And I was free and have remained free from the burden of those sins.

The question might arise, weren't you really forgiven when you confessed those sins to God in the private prayer of your heart? I wholeheartedly believe that I was. But by humbly bringing these to my brother, and to the light, the remaining emotional bond that they had on my conscience was broken. I no longer carry the burden of those sins alone. My brother, who is indwelt by Christ, knows them. And he and Christ still love me! I believe that is why Thomas Gallagher calls confession the gateway of "what God does in response to our request: the loving embrace, the welcoming kiss, the joyful celebration, and the outpouring of new life that we call forgiveness."[104]

May you know the truth of this as well and celebrate! And you can celebrate because as John Baillie says, "And in my heart's most secret chamber you are waiting to meet and speak with me, freely offering me your fellowship in spite of all I have done wrong."[105]

TURNING THE HANDLE TO THE DOOR OF CONFESSION

- You may be reluctant or find it hard to confess. John Baillie understood this and wrote in one of his prayers, "What I was not too ashamed to commit, may I not be too ashamed to confess."[106] To prepare your heart, pray this prayer from the pen of the Puritan:

Give me grace to know more of my need of
grace;
Show me my sinfulness that I may willingly
confess it;
Reveal to me my weakness that I may know
my strength in thee.
I thank thee for any sign of penitence;
give me more of it;
My sins are black and deep,
and rise from a stony, proud, self-righteous
heart;
Help me to confess them with mourning,
regret, self-loathing,
with no pretence to merit or excuse;
I need healing,
Good Physician, here is scope for thee.[107]

- In quiet meditation, examine your life and ask the Holy Spirit to bring to your mind something that you have done that has broken your relationship with another person whether it is a member of your family, a co-worker, a friend, or the person who lives next door. These broken human relationships also mean you have a broken relationship *with God*. What unkind or unjust actions? What untruthful words? What selfishness? Or covetousness? What pride?

  Admit your sinful behaviour and thoughts. Confess them to God without making them less than they are, without excuses or rationalizations. Then go to the person you have sinned against and ask them to forgive you.

  Then you can joyfully enter into the presence of Jesus and revel in his amazing grace and unconditional love.

- Are you plagued with the burden of secret sin from your past? Have you, like the author, confessed it to the Lord but in some way are haunted by it and not able to feel free?

Would you be willing to confess it to a brother or sister in Christ and bring it to the light of the gospel of Jesus?

Pray and think carefully about who you could share with. You should not just share with anyone. Some people may not be spiritually ready or able to participate in this exercise. Therefore, you should choose a person who is godly and well aware of their own sinfulness. They should be someone you trust and who will keep confidence. Once you have chosen the person, approach them to see if they would be willing to hear your confession. Then meet with them. Confess your sins and be forgiven and set free in Jesus's name.

10

The Door of Fasting

Beware of books on fasting.
– John Piper[108]

I had to laugh at that opening sentence of John Piper's book on fasting. I had followed that advice carefully all my life. Yes, I had dipped into them occasionally but never seriously. It wasn't something that I was drawn to or really wanted to practice regularly.

In fact, a number of years ago our mission was approaching a day of prayer and fasting and another missionary and I were discussing our participation, and this colleague said, "I don't fast. It's something I just don't do." I was struck not only by the honesty of that statement but because that was my attitude as well. It was not that I never had fasted. I tried it, but I just couldn't get into it. I didn't seem to get anything out of it – or the time spent in the practice.

I also had a good reason I rationalized. For years, I had been a runner. I ran most days and since I ran, I reasoned that I couldn't fast. In fact, books on running recommend those who run not to fast. How convenient. So, my spiritual life is stunted in this area.

As I have been thinking about fasting the Lord has been impressing upon my mind that my conception is wrong. I have been looking at it from the perspective of fasting *from* something rather than fasting *for* something. Fasting from something is deprivation. Fasting for something is anticipation. Fasting from something has a negative connotation while fasting for something is positive.

It is interesting to see Paul's comments on eating and not eating in Romans 14. The context is about eating or not eating certain foods. Although Paul does not deal with it specifically here, some feel he may be referring to meat offered to idols (see 1 Corinthians 8 for Paul's discussion on meat offered to idols). But in this context, he also speaks of observing special days or not. However, Paul is more interested in motivations of which there are two. One is that we won't let our behaviour be unloving toward the held convictions of another believer. This will be demonstrated by a non-judgmental attitude as seen in verses 10-15.

However, the second motivation is that what we do is for the Lord and we do it with thankfulness. And it is interesting that Paul speaks of this specifically in terms of eating and not eating. We see this in verse 6b: "The one who eats, does so with regard to the Lord, for he gives thanks to God; and the one who does not eat, *it is* for the Lord *that* he does not eat, and he gives thanks to God" (NASB).

If I am fasting for any other reason or motivation other than for the Lord and to use it as an opportunity to thank him then I am fasting with the wrong motivation. I could be like the Pharisees who were fasting to be seen of men, a practice Jesus vigorously condemned.

How do fasting and thanksgiving connect? In my limited experience, I have found that when I fast it is a reminder of my desire to pray. So, I can say, "Thank you, Lord for this person, or that issue and that I can bring them into your presence."

So, applying this thought to fasting, I see that it is not fasting from food and its sensory enjoyment and physical satisfaction, although this is a major part of it. But instead, it is fasting for intimacy with the Lord. Thus, the practice of fasting is like pushing on the door leading into the same room with Jesus. When viewed in this way, I can't ignore why I am not eating. One can't fast mindlessly. It is an act performed as a result of a conscious decision. Therefore, I fast because I want to spend time with Jesus and intentionally enter into an awareness of his presence. This helps me to remember that he is here spiritually even though he is not here in the flesh.

John Piper deals with the whole mystery of Jesus being both here and not here and how fasting can help us with our desire for intimacy with Jesus. He is here in the Spirit and yet that is not "God with skin on" as we mentioned earlier. He says:

> Nevertheless, there is a greater degree of intimacy that we will enjoy with Christ in heaven when this age is over. So in another sense Christ is *not* with us, but away from us. This is why Paul said in 2 Corinthians 5:8 "We would rather be away from the body and *at home with the Lord*"... In other words, in this age there is an ache inside every Christian that Jesus is not here as intimately and powerfully and as gloriously as we want him to be. We hunger for so much more. This is why we fast.[109]

During this past Lenten season, I fasted *from* lunches, but I was fasting *for* a focused time each day to reflect on some aspect of spiritual growth following a daily devotional guide. Some experiences were rich, and others were dry. But it was a first step in practicing the discipline for an extended period of time. That is progress.

I have so much to learn, but there is joy in that. May I encourage you do so as well and enter into the same room as Jesus through this door of fasting and focused time with him?

TURNING THE HANDLE TO THE DOOR OF FASTING

- Reflect on Piper's thought that "there is an ache inside every Christian that Jesus is not here as intimately and powerfully and as gloriously as we want him to be. We hunger for so much more. This is why we fast." What is the relationship between physical hunger experienced during fasting and spiritual hunger? How can fasting lead us to deeper intimacy with Jesus?
- Have you felt led to fast and yet have struggled with carrying it through? What was the point of your struggle? What excuses or rationalizations did you give?
- The next time you feel that you should fast, first examine your motivation. Is it for the Lord and to use it as a means for thankfulness?
- When you feel led to fast do not look at what you are fasting from, but instead identify what you are fasting for. For example, is it wisdom? Is it for clarity in a decision? Is it for a closer relationship with Jesus? Keep this positive God-focused reason in mind as you enter into your fast.

11

The Door of Suffering, Sorrow, and Lament

Are you weary, are you heavyhearted?
Tell it to Jesus, tell it to Jesus.
Are you grieving over joys departed?
Tell it to Jesus alone.

Tell it to Jesus, tell it to Jesus,
He is a friend that's well-known;
You've no other such a friend or brother,
Tell it to Jesus alone.
– Jeremiah Eames Rankin[110]

Suffering is a door into the room where Jesus is. But I have not really experienced it on a deep level. However, I have entered through the door of other people's sorrows and suffering by weeping with those who weep, and by mourning with those who mourn. But I do not demean or desecrate the suffering of others by saying I understand their experience – because I don't. But I can enter their suffering by helping bear their burden as I let their pain, their anguish of heart, and their grief seep into my soul.

The Puritan wrote, "I bless thee . . . for a heart that feels sorrows."[111]

Jesus was a man of sorrows and acquainted with grief and as such if we are going to live with him in this world filled with tragedies, injustice, and sickness our hearts, too, must feel the sorrows of the world in fellowship with him.

Richard Foster raises the question, "What is it about all this sorrow and weeping and mourning? It sounds a bit depressing . . . The old writers, however, had a very different view. They saw it as a gift to be sought after, the 'charism of tears.' *For them the people most to be pitied are those who go through life with dry eyes and cold hearts*" (emphasis mine).[112]

These tears and sorrow are not something that can be conjured up. However, as God works in us to become compassionate like Jesus it can open up the emotional part of our inner being which may have been locked away in our more cerebral orientation to life and ministry. Again, quoting Richard Foster, he says, "I do know that unless the emotive centre of our lives is touched, it is as if a fuse remains unlit. Tears are a sign – not an infallible sign, to be sure, but a sign nevertheless – *that God has touched this centre*" (emphasis mine).[113]

This raises the question, "How can I stay in touch with my emotive centre?" One of the ways for me is not only to practice lament when I encounter injustice, oppression, and tragedy but also in my daily life. And so, I have made it a habit to read the lament Psalms. In these Psalms I see how David and others confront suffering, sickness, and injustice. But they don't internalize the pain, instead they take it to the Lord. For me it means entering into the same room as Jesus and leaving the suffering with him.

But I also have started to read laments that others have written. One particular source is from Ann Weems whose son, Todd, was killed less than an hour after his twenty-first birthday. Part of her grief work was to write out her pain, sorrow, and questions in her book *Psalms of Lament*. In the preface of the book she wrote, "There is no salvation in self-help books; the help we need is far beyond self. Our only hope is to march ourselves to the throne of God and in loud lament cry out the pain that lives in our souls."[114]

Robert Murray McCheyne, the godly, Scottish pastor of the mid-1800s, made the same point when he wrote, "Embrace the whole world, and carry it within the veil."[115] As we engage with evil, suffering, and injustice through lament we carry it within the veil and bring it to the throne of grace to find help and mercy in our time of need (Hebrews 4:16).

Taking the sorrow to Jesus and releasing it is the key in this engagement with our suffering and the suffering of others whether near us or around the world. If we don't tell it to Jesus and then unburden ourselves by casting our burden upon the Lord (Psalm 55:22), we will be in danger of becoming overwhelmed, distressed, and even bitter. Richard Foster counsels us on this matter when he writes:

> We must not continue shouldering the burdens of others, but rather we release them into the arms of the Father. Without this releasing the burdens will become too much for us, and depression will set in. Besides it is not necessary. Our task in reality is a small one: to hold the agony of others just long enough for them to let go of it for themselves. Then together we can give all things over to God.[116]

So, the practice of lament does not make me feel morbid or melancholy. On the contrary it calms my spirit and fills me with joy as my heart is turned to look at God as the righteous judge and the almighty King who is still on his throne. Brian Fairchild comments:

> [In the] Psalms of lament, we are forced to focus on the glory of God . . . We are given the words, the theology, the structures, and the movements with which to lock our gaze upon the glories of God like a heat-seeking missile. Lament does what few other things can do in stripping away lesser focuses.[117]

THE PROCESS OF LAMENT[118]

With this as background, it is necessary for us to look at how we can go through the process of lamenting.

Step One: Sit with the Pain

This is the embracing part of the process that we mentioned earlier. An example of this is in the life of Nehemiah after he heard the walls of Jerusalem were broken down and the gates were burned. In Nehemiah 1:4 we see his response, "When I heard these things, I sat down and wept." And he didn't rush through the mourning process. This sitting with the pain lasted for days before he began his lament. "For some days I mourned and fasted and prayed before the God of heaven. Then I said . . . " (Nehemiah 1:4b-5a).

I don't believe that we can properly enter into the experience or ministry of lament until we allow ourselves to engage with, feel, and embrace the pain for ourselves and for others who are suffering. In my own practice of lament, there are times when I hear of suffering, abuse, and tragedy and I tell my wife, "I want to sit with this for a while," and I allow myself to feel the pain, the sorrow, the horror of it. And then I lament it, and I take it to the Lord, and I turn it over to him.

Recently, in my work in child safeguarding, a colleague shared a child safety report about abuse with me. In my email response to her, I started off by writing a short lament before I began to address the issues she raised. This is how I can maintain wellness. I sit with the pain and then shift the focus to the Lord. Then I can enter into the response work more objectively and less emotionally.

Step Two: Structure of a Lament

Once we have embraced the pain, we are now ready to begin to express the pain. But unfettered expression may not be constructive. Having a structure not only gives opportunity to expansively express one's grief, sorrow, distress, and pain, but also to channel the emotional energy towards a hopeful and helpful state of closure.

We see such a pattern in the book of Lamentations, whereby the individual chapters are based on an acrostic format. This A-to-Z structure forms a boundary for the expression of the lamenting. As Soong-Chan Rah says:

> The chaos that is consistently portrayed in the book of Lamentations finds focus and shape through the acrostic. Lamentations does not hold back its depiction of suffering, and in order to provide a comprehensive account of sufferings, Lamentations employs the help of the acrostic.
>
> Suffering expressed in Lamentations runs deep. Experiencing deep suffering pushes the individual and community in multiple directions, sometimes without constraints. Lamentations' use of the acrostic offers the possibility of full disclosure, but in a safe place . . . Deep suffering can result in a deep despair, unless the boundaries of suffering are laid out.[119]

Not everyone may be inclined to write a lament in an acrostic form. However, the specific form one uses is not important. What is important is that the lament has boundaries and a structure. In the literature, a number of patterns are suggested. However, a possible outline one could use is the following:[120]

- Address to God (Oh God . . .)
- Review of God's faithfulness in the past

- The complaint
- The confession of sin or claim of innocence
- A request for help
- God's response (often what is hoped for)
- A vow to praise, statement of trust in God

Step Three: Share the Lament

Spanish theologian Jon Sobrino said, "All suffering is sacred."[121] We treat it that way when we take it seriously enough to share it with others. However, if we write or practice lament, we must be careful with whom we share it. All may not be ready to enter into the ministry of lament. This may be because of their own pain or their lack of spiritual readiness to enter into this form of intercessory prayer.

Before, I close this chapter, let me share that I have a personal sorrow that I carry which is in the spirit of Paul who says in Romans 9:2, that he has "great sorrow and continual grief" in his heart (NKJV). It is a sorrow that I carry for someone that I love deeply. I wish it would be resolved, and by faith I believe that one day it will be. But until then, it keeps my heart seeking the presence of Jesus. It keeps me coming back into the same room as Jesus. This is a grace and mercy in the midst of my sadness. And, when by God's grace this sorrow is no more, I trust he will allow another to take its place. And that is okay, because it will help keep my heart from becoming cold and hard or indifferent to Jesus.

Ann Weems captures how sorrow takes us into the loving arms and presence of Jesus, Immanuel, God-with-us when she writes:

> Jesus wept
>
> and in his weeping,
>
> he joined himself forever
>
> to those who mourn.

He stands now throughout all time,
    this Jesus weeping,
    with his arms about the weeping ones:
"Blessed are those who mourn,
    for they shall be comforted."
He stands with the mourners,
    for his name is God-with-us.
Jesus wept.[122]

This is significant for those of us who have had a cerebral relationship with Jesus. Life is more than the intellectual and we are more than intellectual beings. Learning to lament and to respond to life with the emotional part of our being opens our soul to enter into a deeper level in our relational relationship with Jesus. In many places in Africa, when someone dies, family and friends come and sit for long periods of time with the bereaved. They do not need to say anything. They just are present with them and in their nearness, they bring comfort. Remember, Jesus is described as "a man of sorrows and acquainted with grief" and as such He understands our sorrows and as he gives us the gift of his presence, we sit in the same room together in the intimacy of suffering.

TURNING THE HANDLE TO THE DOOR OF SUFFERING, SORROW, AND LAMENT

- Richard Foster prays:

    Gracious Jesus, it is easier for me to approach you with my mind than with my tears. I do not know how to pray from the emotive centre of my life or

> even how to get in touch with that part of me. Still, I come to you just as I am . . . Break my stony heart with the things that break your heart.[123]

What situation are you facing now that you need to lament or grieve? Do you feel it has given you the desire to draw near to Jesus? How?

- Or do you feel the situation that you need to lament or grieve is driving you away? Can you explain why?
- Part of lamenting is sitting with the pain. This means allowing yourself to identify, feel, and acknowledge the sorrowful emotions instead of denying or ignoring them. Once you have truly and honestly faced and experienced the emotions then you can take them to Jesus, for he knows, he feels, and he understands what you are going through. This is because he is a man of sorrows and acquainted with grief and he is ready to bind up the wounds of your broken heart. In this way, you can find peace and rest in his presence.

12

The Door of Humility

Before Thee in humility, with Thee in faith,
in Thee in peace.
– Dag Hammarskjöld[124]

This is not a chapter about "Humility, and How I Achieved It." In fact, many of those who have tried to write and explain how one becomes humble have struggled with making it practical. Becoming humble is not a formula such as six simple steps to becoming humble. The truth is that each man or woman must find his or her own way to humility because each person has their own unique hinderances to this virtue's expression in their lives. The heart is desperately wicked. O wretched man that I am![125] Thus, we may desire to be humble but pride, the opposite of humility, constantly inserts its ugly influence in our thoughts, words, and actions.

The English Puritan Richard Baxter describes pride in this way, "O what a constant companion, what a tyrannical commander, what a sly and subtle insinuating enemy is this sin of pride."[126] In contrast, he goes on to say, "Humility is not merely an ornament of a Christian; it is an essential part of the new creature. *It is a contradiction in terms, to be a Christian and not humble*" (emphasis mine).[127] So how does humility become an essential part of who are as followers of Christ?

The apostle Paul in Colossians 3:12 and the apostle Peter in 1 Peter 5:5 tell us that we should clothe ourselves with humility, because as Peter says, "God opposes the proud but shows favour to the humble." And if God opposes the proud person, it definitely is a major obstacle in entering the same room as Jesus. So how does one don the clothing of humility?

Perhaps defining humility first would help. As I have thought about what it is, I believe a simple working definition would be this: "Humility is being content with who I am as God has created me." Humble living is then living within the reality of how God has created us. Thomas Merton makes this point in his chapter on "Being and Doing" when he writes that we should first, "be content to *be* in Him, and to do whatever He wills, according to our limitations."[128] And secondly, that we should "be content with the good will and work that are the quiet expression of our inner life."[129]

Our talents, abilities, personalities, and gifts are just the raw materials, or the clay, which the Potter uses to craft each one of us as a vessel fit for the master's use. The vessel God makes us to be is preparatory for our vocation, or our calling in life. Thus, we are not only to be humbly content with who we are but also with what God has called us to do. The Creator has distinctively designed us for a unique ministry in the body of Christ. In other words, no one else can do what God has planned and ordained for us to do. This is the truth Paul expresses in 1 Corinthians 12:18: "But in fact God has placed the parts in the body, every one of them, just as he wanted them to be."

C. S. Lewis says, "Pride is *essentially* competitive – is competitive by its very nature . . . that is why it goes on and on."[130] However, when I am content with my own uniqueness, I realize I don't have to exalt, or prove myself, or be proud of my gifts, talents, and abilities. Therefore, there should be no pride in who I am, nor any competition with others regarding what I am called to do because both my creation and my calling is a gift from God.

Instead, I should be humbly content and grateful for God's gracious plan for me.

All that I have is only what God has given to me, therefore there is no need to boast. And when I have reached that state, I have clothed myself with humility. Thomas á Kempis emphasizes this when he writes:

> So do not be proud of any skill or knowledge you may have, for such is an awesome responsibility. No matter how much you know, realize how much you do not know. Do not be afraid to acknowledge your own ignorance. Why have an exalted opinion of yourself when you know there are many, even in your own field, whose knowledge surpasses yours? If you want to learn anything worthwhile, seek rather to be unknown and to be thought of as nothing.[131]

The root sin of Satan was pride. We see this in Isaiah 14:12-14:

> How you have fallen from heaven,
>   morning star, son of the dawn!
> You have been cast down to the earth,
>   you who once laid low the nations!
> You said in your heart,
>   "I will ascend to the heavens;
> I will raise my throne
>   above the stars of God;
> I will sit enthroned on the mount of assembly,
>   on the utmost heights of Mount Zaphon.
> I will ascend above the tops of the clouds;
>   I will make myself like the Most High."

Satan was not content with whom God created him to be, and he was not willing to live within the reality of his creaturely attributes and limitations. And in so doing he became the enemy of God through his pride. As C. S. Lewis says, "Pride always means enmity – it *is* enmity."[132] And Satan transmitted this unwillingness to live within his creaturely status to Adam and Eve in the Garden of Eden when he tempted them to reach beyond who they were as creatures so that they would be like God (Genesis 3:5). Thomas Merton discusses humility and pride in this way:

> Christian humility is first of all a matter of supernatural common sense. It teaches us to take ourselves as we are, instead of pretending (as pride would have us imagine) that we are something better than we are. If we really know ourselves we quietly take our proper place in the order designed by God . . . Pride makes us artificial, and humility makes us real.[133]

And Merton continues by saying, "Pride always longs to be unusual. Humility not so."[134]

How pride makes us artificial and longing to be unusual is seen in the contrast between the Pharisee and the tax collector who were praying in the temple:

> The Pharisee stood by himself and prayed: "God, I thank you that I am not like other people – robbers, evildoers, adulterers – or even like this tax collector. I fast twice a week and give a tenth of all I get." But the tax collector stood at a distance. He would not even look up to heaven, but beat his breast and said, "God, have mercy on me, a sinner" (Luke 18:11-13).

If we are prideful, our relationship with Jesus will be artificial and based on our own self-centred self-deception like the Pharisee. "I thank you that I am not like other people!" His thought was, "I am more holy. I am more devoted. I am more (fill in the blank)." He longed to be unusual.

But humility confesses who we are as the penitent publican cried out, "God, have mercy on me, a sinner." He knew he wasn't unusual. He didn't long to be so but instead longed to be forgiven. And in being forgiven he was able to be reconciled with God. Thus, pride is the opposite of humility and hinders our ability to draw near to Jesus because living in pride is living in deception. Humility is living in the truth of who we are and thus we do not come to Jesus with a false presentation of ourselves, but we come to Jesus just as we are. Therefore, Thomas Merton tells us that:

> Sooner or later we must distinguish between what we are not and what we are. We must accept the fact that we are not what we would like to be. We must cast off our false, exterior self like the cheap and show garment that it is. We must find our real self, in all its elemental poverty but also in its very great and very simple dignity: created to be a child of God.[135]

And since we are created as a child of God we are capable of entering into a close and intimate loving relationship with Jesus.

Thomas á Kempis gives us a warning and encouragement to look realistically and humbly at ourselves:

> You are not better for being praised, nor worse for being blamed, for you are what you are, nor will you be more nor less than God sees you to be. If you know what you are within yourself, the opinion of others will not interest you.[136]

And if the opinion of others does not interest us, we can live humbly content in God's creation of who we are and in his plan for our life. As a result, there is no striving or jealousy that motivates us to live artificial lives.

Thus, we see that humility is a door to enter into the same room as Jesus. Our sin of pride will separate us from God. But David says in Psalm 51:17, "a broken and contrite heart you, God, will not despise." Our humble confession of who we are will remove the barrier of pride between us and allow us to be near to Jesus.

TURNING THE HANDLE TO THE DOOR OF HUMILITY

- Take some time to reflect on the humility of Jesus in Philippians 2:1-11. What can you learn for your own development in humble living from his ultimate example of humility?
- Reflect on this thought from C. S. Lewis, "As long as you are proud you cannot know God."[137] Why is this true? In what way, do you see yourself as proud?
- Confess any thoughts or dissatisfaction with your creation or calling or any acts of pride and competition with other members of the body of Christ.
- As you seek to enter into the same room with Jesus take some time to pray the following prayer:

    Lord, thank you for creating me uniquely for a unique purpose and ministry. Help me to be content with how you have created me and with what you have called me to do. Help me to live in contentment with who I am and what I have been called to do for the sake of building of the Kingdom of God.

13

Jesus Knocking on Our Door

The door in God that opens
is the door he knocks at.
– C. S. Lewis[138]

We could not seek God unless He were seeking us.
– Thomas Merton[139]

We have been discussing our movement through various doors into the same room with Jesus. However, in this chapter we are going to turn the metaphor around and look at Jesus coming into the same room with us.

This familiar thought comes from Revelation 3:20 where in the passage Jesus is pictured as standing on the outside and knocking on the door or our heart and he says, "Here I am! I stand at the door and knock. If anyone hears my voice and opens the door, I will come in and eat with that person, and they with me."

Some have understood this verse as speaking of salvation, however, that is not the intended meaning. It is clear that fellowship is in mind. In the culture of that day, as in ours today, eating a meal is a clear picture of spending time and enjoying one another's company. While, today, we may go out to a restaurant with friends, there is something different about sharing a meal in one's home. It is more personal. It is more intimate, and I believe it shows a desire for a deeper level in the relationship.

Thus, when Jesus knocks on the door of our heart it is an indication of how much he desires to have close fellowship with us. I believe we can see the intensity of this longing in what he said to his disciples during the last supper in Luke 22:15, "With *fervent* desire I have desired to eat this Passover with you before I suffer" (NKJV). Just as he eagerly desired to fellowship with his disciples then, he now has that same intensity towards intimacy with us in the inner room of our heart if we will simply open up the door and welcome him to come in.

And yet there are times when Jesus is knocking, and we are not ready to answer the door. We have other people, other plans, other activities, other desires, and many of them good, worthwhile, and valuable, which hinder us from immediately opening the door and welcoming him. Richard of St. Victor, a Scottish monk who lived in the late 1100s, labels making the beloved wait as an insult. He describes the delay as great weariness as he writes:

> How often must one repeat: "Wait and wait again, a moment here and a moment there"? A moment in one place, a moment in another. A moment in the garden, a moment in the great hall . . . until at last finally after much waiting and great weariness He enters . . . and occupies the most intimate and secret place.[140]

Ken Gire's prayer shows how we should respond when Jesus comes and knocks on our heart's door:

> And for those times when you yearn for my fellowship and stand at the door and knock, grant me a special sensitivity to the sound of that knock so I may be quick to my feet. Keep me from letting you stand out in the cold or ever sending you away . . . May my heart be warm and inviting, so that when you do knock, a worthy place will always be waiting.[141]

Joseph Cardinal Bernardin talks about our fellowship with Jesus as the *hospitality of our soul.* When Jesus comes knocking and earnestly desires to come into our heart to have warm and intimate fellowship with us, how hospitable, how welcoming of him are we? Or are there things in our hearts that hinder our hospitality? Are there things that we wouldn't want him to see? When we invite guests into our home for dinner we go through the house and clean and tidy it up. We prepare for their coming so that everything is in order, and when it is, we are free and happy to usher them in and without hesitation we enjoy our time together. Bernardin describes this process of preparation as letting go. He writes:

> By letting go, I mean the ability to release from our grasp those things that inhibit us from developing an intimate relationship with Jesus.
>
> Letting go is never easy. Indeed, it is a lifelong process . . . I have prayed and struggled constantly to be able to let go of things more willingly, to be free of everything *that keeps the Lord from finding greater hospitality in my soul or interferes with my surrender to what God asks of me . . . My daily prayer is that I can open wide the doors of my heart to Jesus and his expectations of me* (emphasis mine).[142]

As we examine our heart prayerfully, we can ask the Holy Spirit to bring to mind those things that we need to let go or to clean up, through confession. In this way we can be ready to throw wide open the door of our heart in a joyful expression of spiritual hospitality in answer to the knocking of Jesus.

Thus, an important question to address is, If Jesus is standing at the door and knocking, what is the knock? What does that sound like? Is it an insistent hammering and banging? Is it an undeniable call for our attention?

It is interesting that as Elijah was in the cave God used an earthquake and fire to make his presence known. But he didn't come to him in the earthquake or the fire. Those events certainly got his attention. But the presence of God was heard in the still small voice.

And so the knocking of God may at times come in the more obvious events and moments of messy upheaval, as perhaps he can get our attention in no other way. But then in the aftermath when our hearts are torn and weary, he may come again with a gentle rapping or tapping. And then, in those quiet moments of loneliness, sadness, or despair that follows the chaos, we hear his voice asking, "May I come in? I want to have fellowship with you and spend time with you in the middle of your turmoil."

Ann Weems eloquently invites Jesus to come in through the door of her heart as she evokes the imagery of advent when she writes:

> O my God, there is an inn in my heart
> Where the door is open to you;
> please come to my misery.
> Please live in my despair.
> Do your birthing in my manger
> so that I may once again
> hear in my heart
> the good news of great joy.[143]

But Jesus doesn't just want to fellowship with us in times of trouble, and thus the knock may be of the friend who is coming for a visit. It is a more quiet and gentle sound as he seeks to get our attention. He is coming for coffee, or tea, and a chat. He earnestly desires this kind of interaction. But he will not barge through the door. Instead, he stands, gently knocking, waiting to be ushered in. Just writing these words makes me want to rush to the door of my heart and say, "Come in! It is so good to see you! I have longed to have you here. Let's share, and laugh, and love on each other, my Brother and my Friend. Will it be coffee or tea?"

TURNING THE HANDLE AS JESUS KNOCKS ON THE DOOR

- What is the status of the hospitality of your soul? Are you ready to invite Jesus in as he stands knocking on the door of your heart? Ask the Holy Spirit to show you what are some things that you need to let go so that he can enter in and have full and free fellowship with you.
- John Woolman, the godly Quaker, records these prayers of his younger sister, Elisabeth, who died of smallpox when she was thirty-one years old. These are expressions of desire and open invitation to intimacy with God. Take time to meditate upon them and when ready use them as a guide to invite Jesus to enter into your inner room and to fellowship with you:

    I. Oh! that my head were as waters, and mine eyes as a fountain of tears, that I might weep day and night, until acquainted with my God.

II. O Lord, that I may enjoy thy presence! or else my time is lost, and my life a snare to my soul.

III. O Lord, that I may receive bread from thy table, and that thy grace may abound in me!

IV. O Lord, that I may be acquainted with thy presence, that I may be seasoned with thy salt, that thy grace may abound in me![144]

14

When Jesus Doesn't Open the Door

One day you were here, O God, and then you disappeared . . . One day we were talking, and suddenly you turned silent.
And I spoke only to the wind.
– *Ann Weems*[145]

I am at a loss to know what thou wouldst have me do, for I feel amazingly deserted by thee, and sense thy presence so little.
– *Arthur Bennett*[146]

In the parsonage of one of the churches I served the front door was made of heavy dark wood. In the centre was a brass mail slot through which the postman would slip our letters, bills, and junk mail. But it was also a means for our neighbour girl, who was three or four years old, to see if we were home or not. Every once in a while, she would come by to visit us. We might not hear her faint knocks and so if we didn't come to open the door, she would push open the slot and call, "Morrison! You there?"

Maybe some of us can identify with this little girl. We knock on the door of the room where we know Jesus is, but he doesn't open the door. We have been there before. We have visited with him and enjoyed his fellowship and the intimacy of a delightful friendship. But now, we knock and there is no answer. And we cry out, "Jesus! You there?"

Ann Weems captures this feeling in her "Lament Psalm Twenty-six." Can you identify with her words of concern about the absence of God's response? But also notice her faith and hope at the end:

> I am on my knees, O God,
> asking for your help,
> but you do not give it.
> I constantly seek you,
> but I do not find you.
> I stand at your door and knock
> but it is not opened to me.
> I'm asking for a fish;
> don't give me a snake.
> I'm asking for an egg;
> don't give me a scorpion.
> I'm hungry
> for your presence,
> O God.
> I'm starving
> for your holiness!
> Even we sinners know
> how to give good gifts
> to our children.
> Give me then, O my God,
> your holy spirit.

O God, I will continue
to ask, to seek, to knock,
for you are the door of hope,
and you will let me in,
and you will say to me:
"I am your God,"
and I will bow down,
and I will receive,
and I will find.

And the door will be
opened to me,
and I will live
in your blessing,
and my mouth
will be forever
full of praise
for my God.[147]

As we think about the absence of God, it might be good to state from the beginning that this feeling is common and is a natural part of the believer's spiritual experience. We see this expressed throughout the Psalms:

> Why, O Lord, do you stand far off? Why do you hide yourself in times of trouble? (Psalm 10:1)

> How long, Lord? Will you forget me forever? How long will you hide your face from me? (Psalm 13:1)

> My God, my God, why have you forsaken me? Why are you so far from saving me? (Psalm 22:1)

> Lord, do not forsake me; do not be far from me, my God. (Psalm 38:21)

> O God, do not keep silent; do not turn a deaf ear,
> do not stand aloof, O God. (Psalm 83:1)

All of these are expressions of spiritual pain and sorrow that God is not present. But even in these expressions of confusion and a lack of understanding God's absence, we can say that in and of themselves they are expressions of the believer's love and deep desire for a closer, more intimate relationship with him. If we do not hunger for God and his presence in our life, do we really love him? Tim Keller, referencing the Puritan John Owen, writes, "Our expressions of grief at the sense of God's absence are themselves ways to show love to God, and they will not go unappreciated by him."[148]

What is interesting is that after the psalmists express their feeling that God was silent, or far away, they go on to pray and bring their concerns to God. Even though God seemed to be absent they continued to trust him for help and comfort. What this points out is that our feeling of God's absence does not change the reality of his presence. Austin Phelps comments on this when he writes:

> A consciousness of the *absence of God* is one of the standing incidents of religious life. Even when the forms of devotion are observed conscientiously, the sense of the presence of God, as an invisible Friend, whose society is a joy, is by no means unintermittent.[149]

This, then, raises the question, why does God seem to be far away when we know he is present with us? Why would the door be closed? Or at least why is there no immediate answer? There may be a number of reasons but let me suggest of few of them.

First, as we have already discussed in chapter 9, on confession, we may have unconfessed sin in our lives. And because of this, Jesus will not answer the door as he waits for us to repent and confess our wrongdoing. But also, over a period of time if we continue to refuse to confess our sin our hearts will grow spiritually hardened; and so while we continue to pray, we will not be hearing the voice of the Father and thus wrong desires and motivations will characterize our requests and petitions. Richard Foster's words are helpful when he writes:

> Our sin, by its very nature, separates us from God, rupturing the intimate fellowship and dulling our spiritual sensitivities. We become nearsighted and develop thickened eardrums, if you will. The result is an inability to discern the heart of God and an asking that is askew. We ask wrongly, to spend it on our passions, as James reminds us (James 4:3). Therefore, our prayers are hindered.[150]

To test this as one possibility as to why Jesus doesn't answer when we knock on the door we can follow the counsel of John Baillie in his prayer when he writes, "And if I still cannot find you, O God, then let me search my heart and know whether it is I who am blind rather than you who are hidden: whether it is I who am running away from you rather than you from me."[151] And if sin is found, we must immediately confess and forsake it before the door will be opened unto us.

Secondly, he may be testing us. There is a very interesting verse about God and his dealing with Hezekiah which says, "God left him to test him and to know everything that was in his heart" (2 Chronicles 32:31). However, because God is all-knowing, it can also be understood that God withdrew so that Hezekiah himself might know all that was in his own heart. This is a hard verse to understand especially to us who hold fast to the promise that Jesus will never leave us nor forsake us. But it does show us why at times we may not feel close to him. The old commentator, Adam Clarke's comments on this passage are very helpful:

> Thus God speaks after the manner of men: he either brings, or permits them to be brought, into such circumstances as shall cause them to show their prevailing propensities; and then warns them against the evils to which they are inclined, after having shown them that they are capable of those evils. To know ourselves, and our own character, is of the utmost importance to our religious growth and perfection . . . Many, by not being fully acquainted with their own character, have been unwatchful and unguarded, and so become an easy prey to their enemies.[152]

Thus, if God seems to have removed himself, it may be a warning to us that God is testing us and thus we should take special heed to ourselves and for any potential temptation that may be coming our way. Hezekiah gave in to the temptation of pride as he displayed the marvels and wealth of his kingdom. We may be tempted in a similar way or in the areas of our own weaknesses. Even if God seems far away, we can still "cast [our] burden on the Lord, and he will sustain [us]" (Psalm 55:22, ESV).

Thirdly, God may be working out his purposes for us or others for his glory, but we may be totally unaware of what he is doing. The psalmist has an interesting picture that he uses to describe the ways of God. Listen to what he says in Psalm 77:19: "Your path led through the sea, your way through the mighty waters, though your footprints were not seen."

Unseen footprints in the water? Footprints indicate presence. You don't have a person's footprints if he or she is not there. We can track someone's footprints in the dirt and dust. But if they are walking in deep water and we want to track them there is no way that we can! So, if God is walking in the deep waters, God is working but we can't see. We don't know what he is doing. Sometimes God's ways are mysterious. God's presence is often an unseen presence. It takes faith to trust the unseen.

How does this apply to us? We may be walking through the deep and mysterious waters of poor health, of financial stress, or of a marriage relationship that is hard and painful, and we are at the point of giving up. We are wondering, "Do you see my need and my struggles? Do you see my heartache? God, where are you?" Or as Ann Weems describes it:

> You did not hear
>   my crying.
> Day after day
>   and night after night,
> I called to you,
>   but you did not answer.
> You slept
>   while I wept.[153]

The answer is that God is with us even when he seems not to be. Thomas Merton explains this seeming paradox when he writes:

> God, who is everywhere, never leaves us. Yet he seems sometimes to be present, sometimes absent. If we do not know him well, we do not realize that he may be more present to us when he is absent than when he is present."[154]

This is because when he is *absent* it increases our conscious awareness of our need of his presence. In fact, when we feel his absence, we cry out to him whom we know is still present!

David expresses some of these struggles in the Psalms:

> How long, Lord? Will you forget me forever?
>   How long will you hide your face from me?
> How long must I wrestle with my thoughts
>   and day after day have sorrow in my heart?
>   (Psalm 13:1-2a)

But David also affirms that God has not abandoned us. God knows and he cares:

> You have searched me, Lord,
>   and you know me.
> You know when I sit and when I rise;
>   you perceive my thoughts from afar.
> You discern my going out and my lying down;
>   you are familiar with all my ways.
> Before a word is on my tongue
>   you, Lord, know it completely.
> You hem me in behind and before,
>   and you lay your hand upon me. (Psalm 139:1-6)

Yes, he is there; trust him that he cares. And he is the one who heals the broken hearted, but at this moment his footprints are unseen. Hold on to this truth: God is at work even though we may not see it or feel his presence. His ways may be hidden and mysterious but his promise that he will never leave us nor forsake us remains true.

Fourthly, God may be growing our faith. Never doubt in the dark what God has revealed to you in the light. This is what the prophet Isaiah counsels the servants of the Lord, in Isaiah 50:10:

> Let the one who walks in the dark,
>   who has no light,
> trust in the name of the Lord
>   and rely on their God.

The alternative is to trust in ourselves and to walk by our own light, but the prophet warns, in the next verse, that it will only lead to our torment:

> But now, all you who light fires
>   and provide yourselves with flaming torches,

> go, walk in the light of your fires
>   and of the torches you have set ablaze.
> This is what you shall receive from my hand:
>   you will lie down in torment.

So, when Jesus doesn't open the door and all seems dark, we have a choice. We can rely on our wisdom, our own light, but which will lead us in the wrong direction to our own personal harm. Or we can wait in faith for God to give us more light so we can continue on the path with confidence.

Let me give an example from my own life which I believe illustrates the mysterious ways of God and that we may not fully understand what God is doing. When I was in seventh grade our family moved from Wisconsin to Pennsylvania. However, after one year my father became unemployed. That was very difficult for me as I saw him struggle for the next year and a half with various part-time and menial jobs just to stitch a living together.

And I asked, "God why did you bring us all the way out here only to have my father lose his job and struggle just to put food on the table for a family of eight?" But now as I look back, I see that God brought us out East for many reasons. However, I believe the main one was for the church we attended. My oldest brother received Christ in that church. I, along with all of my brothers and sisters dedicated our lives to serve the Lord there. And my son did as well many years later. That church also has supported my wife and me as missionaries for all the years of our service. I didn't know all about that when I was twelve years old. The whole situation was mysterious and made no sense. But God was in it, although his footprints were not seen.

So, the proper response in the mystery and the misunderstanding or lack of understanding of what God is doing is to come to a point of faith and trust where we can then follow him no matter where he leads. The Puritan understood this experience and expresses the desire to grow in his faith as he recognizes unbelief has kept him from sensing the presence of Jesus when he writes:

> I often mourn the absence of my beloved Lord
> whose smile makes earth a paradise,
> whose voice is sweetest music,
> whose presence gives all graces strength.
> But by unbelief I often keep him outside my door.
> Let faith give entrance that he may abide with me
> forever.[155]

Andrew Murray in his book *Christ Is All* has a chapter titled "When Christ Sleeps." He tells the story of Jesus falling asleep in the boat as they crossed the Sea of Galilee. The disciples must have felt sure that because Jesus was with them their voyage would be safe and successful. But Jesus fell asleep, and the storm swept down upon them. And they didn't feel the presence of Jesus even though he was right there!

C. S. Lewis says, "The *hiddenness* of God perhaps presses most painfully on those who are in another way nearest to Him."[156] His hiddenness was not a matter of reality – he was in the boat! It was a matter of misunderstanding who he was. This is clearly seen in the question they asked after Jesus awoke and calmed the raging sea. They asked, "What kind of man is this?" They didn't have a category for Jesus who had his *Godness* veiled in human flesh. His presence hidden in plain view.

We close this chapter with Murray's wise counsel as he reflects on this incident in the disciples' training in faith:

> Christ slept in the ship so that he might teach the disciples this precious truth . . . Trust Jesus when he appears to sleep and not to hear. He is still the Almighty One. He is still the Living God . . . *Make it your first priority in your own inner life and in*

your Christian work for and with others, to rest in the presence of Jesus, even when you cannot see him, with the deep restfulness of perfect faith (emphasis mine).[157]

TURNING THE HANDLE WHEN JESUS DOESN'T OPEN THE DOOR

- Ann Weems writes:

  Everywhere I turn,
  Doors are slammed shut,
  O God,
  do not slam the door
  of heaven
  in my face![158]

When this seems to be happening to you, pray this prayer when the door of heaven seems slammed shut and Jesus doesn't seem to answer or to be near:

Speak to my soul, dear Jesus,
Speak now in tend'rest tone;
Whisper in loving-kindness,
"Thou art not left alone."
Open my heart to hear Thee,
Quickly to hear Thy voice,
Fill Thou my soul with praises,
Let me in Thee rejoice.

Speak Thou in softest whispers,
Whispers of love to me,

"Thou shalt be always conqu'ror,
Thou shalt be always free."
Speak Thou to me each day, Lord,
Always in tend'rest tone,
Let me now hear Thy whisper,
"Thou are not left alone."[159]

- Ask God if there is any sin in your life which may be hindering your relationship with the Lord. Spend some time in self-examination and prayer asking the Holy Spirit to reveal actions, attitudes, and thoughts that are separating you from entering in and experiencing the presence of God. Confess to the Lord what he reveals to you and ask forgiveness for them based on the cleansing blood of Jesus.

15

Someone to Help Open the Door

"Do you understand what you are reading?" And he said, "How can I, unless someone guides me?" (Acts 8:30-31 ESV)

I was on a training trip in São Paulo, Brazil. Sometimes these trips affect my sleep and my dreams, and this time was no different. After a vivid dream I woke up and instantly I realized I was given an important message. This is what I wrote in my journal:

São Paulo, Brazil. 2:20 a.m., October 15, 2019

I'm not big into dreams. But there was a man – actually an ascetic looking man – in a robe and sandals. Jan, my wife, and I had been in a service within an ancient chapel and the music was so beautiful that we were overcome and fell to our knees in worship. We were filled with joy as we made our way out. And he met us there and started

> walking with us as we made our way home. I can't remember what he said, but they were words of spiritual direction. He knew Jan and she understood what he was talking about. I did not.
>
> We came to a place where there were books on spiritual life – classics that seemed to be part of my library – which somehow I missed when we were moving back to America. I wanted to gather them up and take them with me. But we had no box to carry them.
>
> As I woke up just now, the first thought that came to my mind was that I needed a spiritual director.

I believe that my soul needed work and I needed someone to help me. I have read a number of spiritual classics in the past, and they were of some help, but I didn't have them now as a resource. And to be honest, those spiritual classics were not enough. I needed someone to give me guidance and direction. And God in his graciousness led me to a spiritual director.

A spiritual director is one who can help open the doors into the room where Jesus is waiting. Thomas Merton writes of the importance of such a guide. This is a long quote, but I believe it is valuable to share it in its entirety.

> It is very helpful to have a spiritual director who will guide our efforts in self-discipline, and although direction is not absolutely necessary, in theory, for a sound spiritual life, there are, nevertheless, in practice many . . . who will never get anywhere without it. Besides the valuable instruction a good director can give us, we also need his [or her] encouragement and his [or her] corrections.

> It is much easier to persevere . . . if we have someone to remind us of the resolutions we have begun to forget. Spiritual direction will protect us, in some measure, against our own instability. The function of the director is to orientate our discipline toward spiritual freedom. It takes a good director to do this, and good directors are rare.[160]

In some of my travels abroad I have stayed in hotels which have big heavy doors. It is always nice to have a doorman assist me upon my arrival by opening the door and thus easing my entrance into the hotel. The doorman does not go up the elevator and into the room with me. But he can help open the door so that I am able to enter in.

In the same way, the spiritual director does not go with us into the room where Jesus is but rather helps to swing open the doors so we can enter and find fellowship with the King of Kings and the Lord of Lords.

Richard Foster says that spiritual directors "are people gifted in discernment, wisdom, and knowledge. Their task is to help people see the footprints of God in their lives and, now and again, to urge them to move in directions that they might not go otherwise."[161] You may have the desire to grow closer to Jesus and to have a deeper and more intimate relationship with him, but may be struggling with the question of how do I move into that wonderful fellowship that I am yearning for? A spiritual director can hear your soul's longing and sense where you are on your journey to the heart of Jesus. And he or she can help to usher you through the doorway into the same room as Jesus. How can he or she do that? There are a number of ways that I have found true in my own experience.

First, I have found that a spiritual director provides an objective evaluation of my spiritual status. I know that my heart is deceitful and that I can feel that I am doing well. In fact, I want to believe that I am making great strides towards spiritual maturity. My spiritual director helps me to see what progress I am making but also helps me to honestly encounter the areas where I am weak. In fact, the very fact that I know I will discuss my spiritual state helps me to be more honest and to bring them up myself in our sessions together.

Secondly, my spiritual director helps me to wrestle with difficult matters. He listens and reflects on what I have written in my journal as I have tried to work through various issues and my questions. Some may be practical while others are more philosophical or theological. Sometimes we find answers; sometimes we leave them unanswered. And my spiritual director has taught me that I should be willing to live with my questions as God may be using them to eventually provide direction as I wait and think them through.

My spiritual director also leads me into the presence of Jesus through times of prayer and silence. We are not afraid of sitting quietly and allowing that stillness to prepare our hearts for encountering our Lord in a more intimate level. At times we have worshipped together listening to music or reading from other pilgrims on the pathway to a deeper spirituality. And my spiritual director has even been willing to listen to confession of the sins of my youth where it has not been possible to go to those I sinned against. And thus, has helped me to find release and freedom in my soul.

There are some things that a spiritual director is not. First, they do not play an authoritarian role in the directee's life. Michael Rose explains:

> The term "direction" can be misleading as it does not mean a surrendering of one's will to another or one's personal responsibility for their own faith journey. Spiritual direction does not seek to provide answers to questions (tell you what to think) but rather to help you ask those questions

in a genuine way and helps you discover answers ("hear" God) for yourself.[162]

Secondly, a spiritual director is not a mentor as mentoring implies helping the mentee to gain certain skills or competencies. Thus, it is more of a transfer of knowledge and ability to perform a certain functions and tasks or fulfil a specified role. Neither is a spiritual director an accountability partner as that relationship implies a mutuality of sharing and being held responsible for choices and actions. However, as one shares with their spiritual director, he or she helps to hold us accountable as we take steps forward spiritual growth. I find that after we have explored a certain discipline or action I naturally want to share if I have been able to follow through or to discuss any difficulties or struggles. I can do that because we have developed a safe and trusting relationship.

In addition, my spiritual director has been able to point me to resources that have helped me to grow in the pursuit of a deeper walk with Jesus and to strengthen my relationship with him. These include books, music, prayers, poems, and liturgies, all of which are helpful aids in my spiritual growth. While many resources are available to provide guidance, not all are suitable or apply to my present need. Having my spiritual director suggest the exact one has enabled me to keep growing.

Ignatius of Loyola wrote *Spiritual Exercises*, a manual for spiritual directors to use in guiding others in their spiritual formation. Avery Dulles's description of the purpose of this book is also an apt one for that of a spiritual director. He says, "The overall purpose is to enable those being directed to 'overcome their disordered inclinations, to be inflamed with the love of God, and to make firm and concrete resolutions about how to follow Christ more closely.'"[163]

I have found this to be true in my time with my spiritual director. I encourage you to find one who can help you to open the door so you can enter into the same room as Jesus.

TURNING THE HANDLE FOR THE ONE WHO WILL HELP IN OPENING THE DOOR

Are you interested in finding a spiritual director? How can you find such a person? Here are some steps:

- Make it a matter of prayer. Share with the Lord, your deep desire to grow and your felt need for someone to help and guide you.
- Ask your pastor or other leaders for help in finding a spiritual director.
- Meet with the prospective spiritual director to explore the possibility of having him or her provide direction.
- If you agree to meet, consider a trial period to determine your comfort and compatibility level.

16

Swinging the Door Wide Open: Living and Serving with Jesus

Whatever you do, do it all for the glory of God."
(1 Corinthians 10:31)

When we lived in Africa there was a mission hospital in our small community. As a result, there were many doctors who would come for a short time to serve on the staff. Often, they would be involved in teaching medical students who came to the hospital on one of their learning rotations. One doctor would start his early morning rounds in a striking way with the residents. Before they would enter the wards and see the patients he would pray, "Lord, we offer up these rounds as an act of worship." You see, he didn't view his work as a doctor as separate from his walk as a disciple. He practiced the presence of Jesus as a living application of what Paul said in 1 Corinthians.

So far in this book we have been looking at being in the same room as Jesus and practicing his presence mostly from a focus on our inner being. However, in this chapter we want to look at moving out of the inner room, while still in the presence of Jesus, into a world that needs his love and healing touch. Spending time alone with Jesus is how we prepare for service with him. If we do not go out of the room where we have enjoyed our personal and intimate fellowship with him, we may very easily become spiritually narcissistic and self-centred. Thus, after fellowship with Jesus in the inner chamber we continue our fellowship by going together into a world that needs the lived-out presence of Jesus in every act and encounter with our fellowmen who are lost and in need.

Let us look at the example of Jesus as he entered the same room as his Father before he spent time with the people and in his ministry. In Mark 1:35 we read, "Very early in the morning, while it was still dark, Jesus got up, left the house and went off to a solitary place, where he prayed." Notice, this was after a full day of teaching, healing, and driving out demons. And now, before he embarks on another day of travel and preaching, he is spending time with his Father! What Jesus did, so should we. But how did he do it?

It wasn't easy and it didn't just happen, but it was a priority for him.

I believe he had to **plan** for this time for prayer. I don't know what he used for an alarm, perhaps his ear was attuned to the rooster's crowing. But he planned to get up early while no one else was around so that he could be alone and spend time with his Father.

Not only did he plan for it, but he had to find a **place** where he could fellowship. He was in a small house in a small town with his disciples and Peter's family members and the multitudes of those who packed the city looking for Jesus. So, he went out to a solitary place where he would not be interrupted.

In this way, he **protected** his fellowship time. He might have found a place in the corner of the rooftop but soon he would have been discovered. Even when he was out alone, people were searching for him as we see when Peter and the others found him and "they exclaimed: 'Everyone is looking for you'" (Mark 1:37)! In all of this we see Jesus's intentionality to initiate intimacy with his Father. For out of that intimacy flowed power and a commitment to obey his Father's will. Ken Gire puts it this way:

> Jesus's life flowed out of his relationship with the Father. Jesus lived listening to his Father and being obedient to his leading. If the Father was leading him into the wilderness, he went. If the Father wanted him to go to a well in Samaria or to the pool of Bethesda, he went. And if his heavenly Father willed him to go where no earthly father could ever conceive sending a son – to a shameful cross on a brutal hill – he would go there too.[164]

In the same way, our life and service must flow out of our relationship with him. Ministry depends upon our being with Jesus.

This is clearly seen as Jesus was preparing his disciples for their ministry before his ascension. In Matthew 28:16-20, where most often the focus is on the Great Commission, there is embedded some important teaching about living and serving with Jesus that we should not miss. In verse 16 we see that "the eleven disciples went to Galilee, to the mountain where Jesus had told them to go." It was a simple command, yet it took some effort for them to travel from Jerusalem to meet him there. They had to go. Without obedience there would have been no blessing of being with Jesus. Then while in his presence, he gave them his commission, "Go and make disciples." But that service was not to be done in their own strength or on their own. They were to go in the power that comes through his assured presence as he said, "And surely I am with you always, to the very end of the age." To summarize we see that they obeyed the command to go to Galilee to be *in* his presence. They would obey the Great Commission *with* his presence.

A. W. Tozer vividly describes this being with Jesus and its impact on service when he writes:

> The spiritual giants of old were men who at some time became acutely conscious of the real presence of God and maintained that consciousness for the rest of their lives . . . The essential point is, *they experienced God.* How otherwise can the saints and the prophets be explained? How otherwise can we account for the amazing power for good they have exercised over countless generations?[165]

They understood the truth of what Jesus said, "Without me you can do nothing." Without living and serving in the presence of Jesus we cannot produce fruit that will last. Our service will not accomplish that which has the character of eternity in it.

Again, quoting from A. W. Tozer we see practically how we can serve in the conscious awareness of the presence of Jesus:

> We must offer all our acts to God and believe that he accepts them. Then hold firmly to that position and keep insisting that every act of every hour of the day and night be included in the transaction. Keep reminding God in our times of private prayer that we mean every act for his glory; then supplement those times by a thousand thought-prayers as we go about the job of living. Let us practice the fine art of making every work a priestly ministration. Let us believe that God is in all our simple deeds *and learn to find him there* (emphasis mine).[166]

This closes the circle. We enter into his presence because we are weak and powerless and our hearts hunger for intimacy with him. But as we draw closer to him, and our hearts beat with his, we are touched with what touches his heart. We are moved with what moves his heart, our will merges with his will, and his work becomes our work. And then together, we go forth with good news and good works to bring the lost and suffering into the family of God.

TURNING THE HANDLE AND SWINGING THE DOOR WIDE OPEN FOR SERVING WITH JESUS

Richard Foster warns, "Service and spirituality go hand in hand, the active life and the contemplative life should never be separated. It is a hard lesson for us to learn. We seem constantly to swing from one extreme of the pendulum to the other." He goes on to say that we all need to learn "that spirituality and service are inseparable twins."[167]

- Evaluate your service and your inner spiritual life. Is there a balance between doing and being? If not, which is more prominent? Think through why this is true. Is there a correction needed?

- If your service and spiritual life are imbalanced what steps can you take to make sure that you are not only abiding in the same room as Jesus but are also actively serving in the world through the power of the presence of Jesus? What needs to be changed to make this a reality?

17

No More Doors: In the Same Room as Jesus

In my Father's house are many rooms . . .
that where I am you may be also.
(John 14:2-3, ESV)

One morning I read the story of Moses going up to the top of Mount Pisgah where the Lord showed him the Promised Land right before his death. I wondered what that last person-to-person encounter might have been like. What details did God disclose to Moses as he described the land he was giving to his chosen people? God had shown Moses his glory, now he was showing him the fulfilment of his promise. It was a gift. A gracious and compassionate conversation with his servant with whom he had so many face-to-face talks. And it was to be their last one on earth because then Moses died. And then Moses was in the presence of God again and their conversation continued.

Then I read, "Since that time no prophet has risen in Israel like Moses, *whom the Lord knew face to face*" (Deuteronomy 34:10, NASB, emphasis mine). As I read these amazing words

I was struck by an intense – almost overwhelming – feeling. It was really a longing to see Jesus face-to-face! Moses had a rare privilege, a unique one, of seeing God and knowing God's presence face-to-face which no one has ever had since then.

Adam and Eve had it before the fall. Enoch walked with God and Moses knew the Lord face-to-face. This is how God intended our relationship to be, but sin destroyed the possibility and the reality of it. But there is a glorious hope! One day we will see Jesus face-to-face! Revelation 22:3-4a says:

> No longer will there be any curse. The throne of God and the Lamb will be in the city, and his servants will serve him. *They will see his face* (emphasis mine).

The curse of separation by sin will be gone. Our lost Eden fellowship, with its perfect intent of a face-to-face relational relationship will be restored and we will see Jesus and be in his physical and real presence forever!

Carrie Ellis Breck wonderfully captures this joyful thought in the following words:

> Face to face with Christ, my Saviour,
> Face to face – what will it be,
> When with rapture I behold Him,
> Jesus Christ Who died for me?
>
> Face to face – oh, blissful moment!
> Face to face – to see and know;
> Face to face with my Redeemer,
> Jesus Christ Who loves me so.
>
> Face to face I shall behold Him,
> Far beyond the starry sky;
> Face to face in all His glory,
> I shall see Him by and by![168]

A Final Prayer

Ken Gire writes a prayer which I find fitting for closing this book:

> Thank you for all the intimate moments we spend together. I know they mean as much to you as they do to me . . . Help me to understand that only a few things really are necessary in life. And when you get right down to it, only one: to sit at your feet . . . listening . . . looking into your eyes . . . and loving you.
>
> Thank you for the privilege of sitting at those nail-scarred feet. Grant me the grace never to regard that privilege casually, nor to neglect it, but to come there humbly, and to come there often . . . because you are worthy to be adored, O beautiful Saviour . . . because you are worthy to be adored.[100]

Endnotes

1. Richard Foster, *Prayer* (San Francisco: HarperSanFrancisco, 1992), 77.
2. Arthur Bennett, ed. *The Valley of Vision: A Collection of Puritan Prayers & Devotions* (Carlisle, Pennsylvania: The Banner of Truth Trust, 2006), 85.
3. Arthur Bennett, *The Valley of Vision*, 403.
4. Augustine, *The Confessions of St. Augustine* (Dover Thrift Editions), Dover Publications. Kindle Edition. Location 171.
5. Richard Foster, *Prayer*, 127.
6. C. S. Lewis, *Letters to Malcolm, Chiefly on Prayer* (New York: Harper Collins, 1992), 151.
7. Dietrich Bonhoeffer, John W. Doberstein, trans. *Life Together* (New York: Harper & Brothers, 1954), 23.
8. Sue Spencer, *African Creeks I Have Been Up* (New York: David McKay Company, Inc. 1963), 10.
9. Arthur Bennett, *The Valley of Vision*, 333.
10. A. W. Tozer, *The Divine Conquest* (Harrisburg, Pennsylvania: Christian Publications, Inc., 1950), 26.
11. A. W. Tozer, *The Divine Conquest*, 107.
12. As quoted by Timothy M. Gallagher, *The Examen Prayer* (New York: The Crossroad Publishing Company, 2006), 10-11.
13. A. W. Tozer, *The Pursuit of God* (Harrisburg, Pennsylvania: Christian Publications, Inc., 1948), 54.
14. As quoted by Timothy Keller, *Prayer: Experiencing Awe and Intimacy with God* (New York: Penguin Books, 2014), 47.
15. As quoted by Richard Foster, *Prayer*, 32.
16. Ray and Anne Ortlund, *In His Presence* (Eugene, Oregon: Harvest House Publishers, 1995), 28.

17. Ray and Anne Ortlund, *In His Presence*, 65.
18. Richard Foster, *Prayer*, 34.
19. Thomas O. Chisholm, "Living for Jesus" in *The Hymnal for Worship and Celebration* (Waco, Texas: Word Music, 1986), 372.
20. Richard Foster, *Prayer*, 162.
21. As quoted by Richard Foster, *Prayer*, 32.
22. Timothy Keller, *Prayer*, 165.
23. John 6:68. Adapted from the Amplified Version.
24. C. S. Lewis, *Letters to Malcolm, Chiefly on Prayer*, 14.
25. Andrew Murray, *Christ Is All* (London: Marshall Pickering, 1990), 12-29.
26. Henry Wadsworth Longfellow, "The Children's Hour" in David L. George, ed., *The Family Book of Best Loved Poems* (Garden City, New York: Hanover House, 1952). 148-149.
27. Richard Foster, *Prayer*, 141.
28. Arthur Bennett, *The Valley of Vision*, 129.
29. Arthur Bennett, *The Valley of Vision*, 41.
30. Thomas Merton, *No Man Is an Island* (New York: Harcourt Brace & Company, 1983), 112.
31. Walter Isaacson, *Leonardo Da Vinci* (New York: Simon & Schuster, 2017), 4.
32. A. W. Tozer, *The Pursuit of God*, 107.
33. Larry Bossidy and Ram Charan, *Execution: The Discipline of Getting Things Done* (New York: Crown Business, 2002), 19.
34. A. W. Tozer, *The Divine Conquest*, 22.
35. Richard Foster, *Celebration of Discipline*, rev. ed. (San Francisco: HarperSanFrancisco, 1988), 105.
36. A. W. Tozer, *The Pursuit of God*, 91.
37. Thomas Merton, *No Man Is an Island*, 112.
38. Thomas Merton, *No Man Is an Island*, 111, 112.
39. "Morning Prayer," https://www.northumbriacommunity.org/offices/morning-prayer/, accessed December 2, 2020.
40. Richard Foster, *Celebration of Discipline*, 3-4.
41. Arthur Bennett, *The Valley of Vision*, 68.
42. Dag Hammarskjöld, *Markings*, Leif Sjöberg and W. H. Auden, translators (New York: Alfred A. Knopf, 1964), 127.
43. Thomas Merton, *No Man Is an Island*, 113-114.
44. Leopold Stokowski, "Leopold Stokowski: 'Musicians Paint Their Pictures on Silence'", *Big Think* (December 5, 2014), https://bigthink.com/words-of-wisdom/leopold-stokowski-musicians-paint-their-pictures-on-silence/, accessed April 21, 2023.

45. Will Hermes, "The Story Of '4'33"'," https://www.npr.org/2000/05/08/1073885/4-33, accessed April 11. 2020.
46. Kevin Grenior, "On Simplicity & Guilelessness," http://ccca.biola.edu/lent/2020/#day-mar-28, accessed March 28, 2020.
47. As quoted in Richard Foster, *Prayer*, 102.
48. Isaac Watts in A. W. Tozer, ed. *The Christian Book of Mystical Verse* (Harrisburg, Pennsylvania: 1963), 1.
49. David Bruce, "Pop Music's Problem with Silence," https://www.youtube.com/watch?v=MUbbNqyLE3Q, accessed April 12, 2020.
50. Ann Weems, *Psalms of Lament* (Louisville, Kentucky: Westminster John Knox Press, 1995), 42.
51. Tish Warren, *Liturgy of the Ordinary* (Downers Grove, Illinois: InterVarsity Press, 2016), 28.
52. John Woolman, *John Woolman's Journal* (from the Christian Classics Ethereal Library. n.d.), 106.
53. Richard Foster, *Prayer*, 116.
54. A. W. Tozer, *The Divine Conquest*, 24
55. A. W. Tozer, *The Pursuit of God*, 52.
56. Clara Tear Williams, *Satisfied*, 1875, https://hymnary.org/text/all_my_life_i_had_a_longing, accessed April 21, 2023.
57. C. S. Lewis, *Letters to Malcolm, Chiefly on Prayer*, 101.
58. Brother Lawrence, *The Practice of the Presence of God* (Nashville, Tennessee: Abingdon Press, 1975), 13
59. John Baillie, *A Diary of Private Prayer* (New York: Scribner, 2014), 47.
60. Arthur Bennett, *The Valley of Vision*, 50.
61. Douglas Kaine McKelvey, *Every Moment Holy* (Nashville, Tennessee: Rabbit Room Press, 2019), xv.
62. Andrew Murray, *Christ Is All*, 71.
63. Dag Hammarskjöld, *Markings*, 92.
64. Douglas Kaine McKelvey, *Every Moment Holy*, 71.
65. C. S. Lewis, *Letters to Malcolm, Chiefly on Prayer*, 119-120.
66. Thomas Merton, *No Man Is an Island*, 32-33.
67. Thomas Merton, *No Man Is an Island*, 33.
68. Augustine, *The Confessions of St. Augustine*, Location 3212.
69. John Baillie, *A Diary of Private Prayer*, 119.
70. C. S. Lewis, *Letters to Malcolm, Chiefly on Prayer*, 75.
71. "Fairest Lord Jesus," https://www.hymnal.net/en/hymn/h/175, accessed April 21, 2023.
72. "noam," *Brown-Driver-Briggs Hebrew and English Lexicon*, https://biblehub.com/hebrew/5278.htm, accessed April 23, 2020.

73. John Baillie, *A Diary of Private Prayer*, 57.
74. Plato, *The Republic*, Benjamin Jowett, trans. Kindle Edition. Location 1132.
75. Ska is Jamaica's first indigenous urban pop style which evolved in the late 1950s from an early Jamaican form of rhythm and blues that emulated American rhythm and blues, especially that was produced in New Orleans, Louisiana. (Dermot Hussey, Encyclopædia Britannica, s. v. "Ska," [https://www.britannica.com/art/ska, accessed July 8, 2020]).
76. Richard Foster, *Prayer*, 11.
77. Andrew Peterson in Douglas Kaine McKelvey, *Every Moment Holy*, xiv-xv.
78. Brother Lawrence, *The Practice of the Presence of God*, 26.
79. Arthur Bennett, *The Valley of Vision*, 191.
80. Arthur Bennett, *The Valley of Vision*, 244.
81. John Baillie, *A Diary of Private Prayer*, 63.
82. Arthur Bennett, *The Valley of Vision*, 31.
83. https://missionbibleclass.org/songs/english-songs/bible-songs/read-your-bible-pray-every-day-song/, accessed April 21, 2023.
84. Richard Foster, *Prayer*, 145-146.
85. Richard Foster, *Prayer*, 137.
86. Walter Kaiser, "Preaching Christ from the Old Testament: Jesus in Every Scripture," https://www.christianitytoday.com/edstetzer/2014/february/preaching-christ-from-old-testament-jesus-in-every-scriptur.html.
87. A. W. Tozer, *The Pursuit of God*, 81.
88. Richard Foster, *Prayer*, 146.
89. Ignatius of Loyola, Louis J. Puhl, trans. *The Spiritual Exercises of St. Ignatius* (New York: Vintage Books, 2000), 41.
90. Richard Foster, *Prayer*, 108.
91. Timothy Keller, *Prayer: Experiencing Awe and Intimacy with God* (New York: Penguin Books, 2014), 80.
92. C. S. Lewis, *Letters to Malcolm, Chiefly on Prayer*, 111.
93. John Woolman, *John Woolman's Journal* (London: J. M. Dent & Songs Ltd., n.d.), 132, Kindle.
94. Thomas Merton, *No Man Is an Island*, 205.
95. Austin Phelps, *The Still Hour; or Communion with God* (Minneapolis, Minnesota: Curiosmith, 2011), 43.
96. Dietrich Bonhoeffer, *Life Together*, 112.
97. Arthur Bennett, *The Valley of Vision*, 37.
98. C. S. Lewis, *Letters to Malcolm, Chiefly on Prayer*, 24.

99. George Herbert, as quoted by Timothy M. Gallagher, *The Examen Prayer*, 90.
100. Dietrich Bonhoeffer, *Life Together*, 115.
101. Arthur Bennett, *The Valley of Vision*, 81.
102. William F. Arndt and F. Wilbur Gingrich, *A Greek-English Lexicon of the New Testament and Other Early Christian Literature*, 2nd ed. (Chicago: The University of Chicago Press, 1979), 368.
103. Dietrich Bonhoeffer, *Life Together*, 111-112.
104. Thomas Gallagher, *The Examen Prayer*, 92.
105. John Baillie, *A Diary of Private Prayer*, 13.
106. John Baillie, *A Diary of Private Prayer*, 45.
107. Arthur Bennett, ed., "The Personal Touch," in *The Valley of Vision: A Collection of Puritan Prayers and Devotions*, (Edinburgh, UK: The Banner of Truth Trust, 1975) https://dokumen.pub/the-valley-of-vision-9780851512280-9781848712034-9781848712027.html, 149.
108. John Piper, *A Hunger for God* (Wheaton, Illinois: Crossway Books, 2013), 13.
109. John Piper, *A Hunger for God*, 40.
110. Jeremiah Eames Rankin, "Tell it to Jesus" in *Inspiring Hymns* (Grand Rapids, Michigan: Singspiration Sacred Music Publishers, 1951), 453.
111. Arthur Bennett, *The Valley of Vision*, 27.
112. Richard Foster, *Prayer*, 39.
113. Richard Foster, *Prayer*, 41.
114. Ann Weems, *Psalms of Lament*, xvi.
115. Andrew A. Bonar, *Memoirs of McCheyene*, (Chicago: Moody Press, 1948), 112.
116. Richard Foster, *Prayer*, 224.
117. Brian Fairchild, "A Plea for Pastors to Preach Psalms of Lament," https://www.tms.edu/blog/preach-psalms-of-lament/, accessed April 8, 2019.
118. The section on "The Process of Lament" first appeared in my book, *Staying On Course: Self-Care for Child Safety Workers* (Morrison, 2019) which is available on Amazon and in the Kindle format.
119. Soong-Chan Rah, *Prophetic Lament: A Call for Justice in Troubled Times* (Downers Grove, Illinois: InterVarsity Press, 2015), 112.
120. Adapted by Gisela Roth from "Trauma Healing" workshop n.d.
121. Jon Sobrino as quoted by Kathleen M. O'Connor, *Lamentations and the Tears of the World* (Maryknoll, New York: Orbis Books, 2002), 106.
122. Ann Weems, *Psalms of Lament*, xxi.
123. Richard Foster, *Prayer*, 46.

124. Dag Hammarskjöld, *Markings*, 104.
125. Paraphrased from Jeremiah 17:9 and Romans 7:24. See also Romans 7:14-25.
126. Richard Baxter, *The Reformed Pastor* (New York: American Tract Society, n.d.), 205.
127. Richard Baxter, *The Reformed Pastor*, 213.
128. Thomas Merton, *No Man Is an Island*, 120.
129. Thomas Merton, *No Man Is an Island*, 121.
130. C. S. Lewis, *Mere Christianity* (San Francisco: Harper San Francisco, 2001), 121-122.
131. Thomas á Kempis, *The Imitation of Christ* (New York: Catholic Book Publishing Co., 1977), 16.
132. C. S. Lewis, *Mere Christianity*, 124.
133. Thomas Merton, *No Man Is an Island*, 113.
134. Thomas Merton, *No Man Is an Island*, 114.
135. Thomas Merton, *No Man Is an Island*, 203.
136. Thomas á Kempis, *The Imitation of Christ*, 84.
137. C. S. Lewis, *Mere Christianity*, 124.
138. C. S. Lewis, *Letters to Malcolm, Chiefly on Prayer*, 25.
139. Thomas Merton, *No Man Is an Island*, 231.
140. Richard of St. Victor as quoted in Richard Foster, and Emilie Griffin, eds., *Spiritual Classics* (New York: Harper Collins Publishers, 2000), 185.
141. Ken Gire, *Intimate Moments with the Savior: Learning to Love* (Grand Rapids, Michigan: Zondervan Publishing House, 1989), 7.
142. As quoted by Timothy M. Gallagher, *The Examen Prayer*, 153-154.
143. Ann Weems, *Psalms of Lament*, 37.
144. John Woolman, *John Woolman's Journal*, 51-52.
145. Ann Weems, *Psalms of Lament*, 83.
146. Arthur Bennett, *The Valley of Vision*, 180.
147. Ann Weems, *Psalms of Lament*, 51-52.
148. Timothy Keller, *Prayer*, 161.
149. Austin Phelps, *The Still Hour*, 7-8.
150. Richard Foster, *Prayer*, 184.
151. John Baillie, *A Diary of Private Prayer*, 109.
152. Adam Clarke, *Commentary and Critical Notes, Vol. II* (New York: 1832), 589-590.
153. Ann Weems, *Psalms of Lament*, 86.
154. Thomas Merton, *No Man Is an Island*, 237.
155. Arthur Bennett, *The Valley of Vision*, 197.

156. C. S. Lewis, *Letters to Malcolm, Chiefly on Prayer*, 60.
157. Andrew Murray, *Christ Is All*, 12-13.
158. Ann Weems, *Psalms of Lament*, 15.
159. L. L. Pickett, "Speak to Me, Jesus" in *Songs That Live* (Harrisonburg, Virginia: Park View Press, 1970), 203.
160. Thomas Merton, *No Man Is an Island*, 112-113.
161. Richard Foster, *Prayer*, 252-253.
162. Michael Rose, "The difference between Coaching and Spiritual Direction?", https://iamsignificant.ca/significant-sustenance/coaching-spiritual-direction/, accessed July 24, 2014.
163. Avery Dulles in Ignatius of Loyola, *The Spiritual Exercises of St. Ignatius*, xvii.
164. Ken Gire, *Intimate Moments with the Savior: Learning to Love*, 127.
165. A. W. Tozer, *The Divine Conquest*, 26-27.
166. A. W. Tozer, *The Pursuit of God*, 123.
167. Richard Foster, *Spiritual Classics*, 209.
168. Carrie E. Breck, "Face to Face," *The Hymnal for Worship and Celebration*, (Waco, Texas: Word Music, 1986), 549.
169. Ken Gire, *Intimate Moments with the Savior: Learning to Love*, 144.

More Books By Philip E. Morrison

Philip E. Morrison moved to Kenya 25 years ago. As a lecturer at Moffat Bible College, he became passionate about equipping under-resourced pastors who are responsible for multiple congregations.

As a result, he founded The Multi-Church Pastor Institute to mentor and train these pastors. In addition to *The Multi-Church Pastor*, he is the author of:

INFLUENCE: LEADING WITHOUT POSITION
Philip E. Morrison & Hankuri Tawus Gaya
Do you have ideas for how to change your community, church, or nation – but feel powerless to make them happen? This book tells you how you can influence others to take action and start change, just as young men and women in the Bible did.

CONFLICT RESOLUTION IN THE CHURCH
Philip E. Morrison with Chris Mwalw'a
This book is an answer to the great need the church has for a practical approach to conflict resolution in the church. It focuses on scripturally-based, peace-making attitudes within the African church context.

FALLING ASLEEP IN THE LAP OF DELILAH
Philip E. Morrison
Falling Asleep in the Lap of Delilah is a treasure trove of wisdom on finishing the race of life well. Facing the final stages of life, career, or ministry can be daunting and instil deep fear. Morrison's thoughtful insights and powerful mediations on the life of Samson can guide you in preserving your relationship with God and with others.

Our mission is to grow discipleship through publishing African voices.

Go to oasisinternationalpublishing.com to learn more.

THE SISTERHOOD SECRET
Levina Mulandi
In this book, Dr Mulandi shows how discipling is more than Bible study or a church program. She shares how she empowers any woman to mentor younger women, guiding them to understand their identity, discern the purpose of their lives, and be transformed to be more like Christ.

HAPPILY WHENEVER AFTER
Bookie Adekanye
Candid and kind, Bookie Adekanye reminds you of God's overwhelming love for you. No matter how society labels you, God says you belong to him. You're invited to heal from past scars and be your confident, courageous self. The God of the Bible used single ladies to deliver and save, and he definitely has a plan for you.

BAESICS
Ernest Wamboye with Waturi Wamboye
In Baesics, Ernest and Waturi Wamboye give no-nonsense advice on how to build a fulfilling love life and marriage. Young adults in African cities feel marriage is priority but are often unprepared. Baesics addresses the relationship dilemmas many young adults are facing today from a Christian point of view.

GETTING MARRIED?
Chao Tsuma Wanje and James Wanje
Written as a friendly and light-hearted conversation, this book is perfect for you and your fiancé(e) to read and discuss together. Drawing from timeless wisdom and real-life examples, this husband-and-wife team helps couples to resolve conflicts before they explode.

THE DIVORCE DILEM
Ron Misiko & Ray Mot
The authors share the experiences as pastors and as married people well as their areas of expertise in the legal system and Bible scholarship. From the different African conte they explain how to navigate the challeng we face today with biblical and practical solutions for divorce c in African churches.

I ONCE WAS DEAD
Cedric Kanana with Benjamin Fischer
This book's riveting, action-packed plot, has one central message shining through: Jesus is stronger than death, than addiction, than Islam, than traditional religion, than curses. Trust Jesus alone! The miracles recorded in I Once Was Dead echo the book of Acts and give all glory to God – whether healing, deliverance, resurrection, protection from threats, or hearing God's voice.

THE GIRL WITH SPECIAL SHOES
Hilda Bih Muluh
Hilda's family didn't know she had muscular dystrophy. They just knew their preschooler was losing her ability to walk. But they were determined to find a cure. *The Girl with Special Shoes* is the witty and heartfelt story of a family's sacrificial love and a God who refashions pain into purpose.

A PRE-MARRIAGE COUNSELLING HANDBOOK
Alan & Donna Goerz
This handbook was written specifically for the African context on how to build a successful marriage. Designed as a seminar-in-a-book, *A Pre-Marriage Counselling Handbook* equips pastors and counselors to teach biblical pre-marriage classes and seminars.

ANSWERS FOR YOUR MARRIAGE
Bruce and Carol Britten
Offers practical insights to marriage issues and facts on sex, pregnancy, family planning, child-raising, money issues, adultery, HIV, and sex-related diseases. If your marriage is in despair, look to this book for some answers for your marriage.

HIGHLY FAVOURED: POWERFUL GOD'S COVENANT WITH YO
Stuart J. Foster
The God of the Bible i unreliable or inaccess like the spiritual being African traditional religions. He chooses have a covenant relationship with his people and we do not have to earn God's fav

oasisinternationalpublishing.com | oasisinternational.co